10-

N

14/15

Leonard, Duval,
Woods and Mickelson

MASTERS OF
THE MILLENNIUM

The Next Generation of the PGA Tour

by
Robert Hartman

a **SPORTS**MASTERS book

a division of Sports Publishing Inc.
www.SportsPublishingInc.com

© 1999 Robert Hartman
Director of Production: Susan M. McKinney
Cover design: Scott Muncaster
Editor: David Hamburg

ISBN: 1-58382-038-8

A SportsMasters Book
SPORTS PUBLISHING INC.
804 N. Neil
Champaign, IL 61820
www.sportspublishinginc.com

Printed in the United States.

To Ryan Bradford and Emma Catherine.

———————————————

CONTENTS

ACKNOWLEDGMENTS

*Everything I ever really needed to know about life
I learned in junior golf.*

The *Masters of the Millennium* officially began in 1981. At the age of seventeen I played in the Western Junior at Ohio State and came to a startling realization. My junior golf game did not belong on the same fairway as some of the other kids playing the Scarlet and Gray courses. I often reflect on the results from those two hot summer days in southern Ohio. I played the same course as other kids in the tournament like Clark Burroughs, Andrew Magee and Skip Kendall, but my game was on an entirely different landscape. I might hold a course record in the Western Junior, the biggest margin from day one to day two. I shot 90-75 and missed the match-play cut by fourteen strokes. I left my clubs in the trunk of my red 1975 Mustang for one month, which signaled the official end of my junior golf career. Meanwhile Magee, Burroughs and Kendall went on to play big-time college golf and eventually the PGA Tour. Humbled, I traveled down the road to big little Hillsdale College.

I played golf for three years (1982-1984) at Hillsdale College in Hillsdale, Michigan. Back then, Hillsdale was an NAIA school that competed in the Great Lakes Intercollegiate Athletic Conference (GLIAC). The school no longer has a golf team. I can only guess that the lack of a home course (Lake Baw Beese Country Club only had 9 holes) contributed to its now defunct status. In the classroom, Hillsdale taught me about independence. English professors Dr. James Juroe and George Oetgen shaped my outlook on life, sports, and most of all, writing.

The clubs I used at Hillsdale, Top-Flite tour blades, I purchased on the recommendation of Jeff Roth at Wabeek Country Club in Bloomfield Hills, Michigan. Roth is not really known as my teacher. He is better known as the fight referee in the parking lot at the PGA Championship when his father accused John Daly of hitting into him. Roth remains an outstanding player, but Bob Percy deserves credit as my junior golf instructor. PGA professional Steve Horvat and current pro Tom Fortuna also provided direction.

A special thanks to Jim Timmerman at Orchard Lake Country Club for an opportunity to shave dew off greens and cut cups. I learned that hard work is sometimes rewarded in many different ways—like the beautification of the playing field.

I would like to thank my parents, Bill and Pat Hartman for teaching me a love for the game and providing me an opportunity to play junior golf, the lessons at Carl's Golfland, the junior clubs and the patience. I am 35 years old and proud to say that I still can't beat my father on the course. My mother deserves credit for not only making sure that I didn't miss any tee-times, but showing me my golf score really was not all that important. We lived behind the fourth hole, but I learned a lot about myself on the seventh hole at Wabeek, Nicklaus wanted it that way.

To Bill, Jim and Sue, even though you're all starting your own foursomes, it will be our foursome in the 1970s that I cherish most. And Matt, congratulations, but your family is still away.

And while 1981 was the official end of my junior golf days, it was the summer of 1987 that inspired this book. From Mission Hills to Meridian; from Otter Creed to Innisbrook, the integrity of the game of golf was about kids with guts, smiles and respect. Some of the players who have made it to the PGA and LPGA Tours like Phil Mickelson, Justin Leonard, Jim Furyk, Michelle McGann, Kelly Robbins were just kids with great golf games back then. But it was the kids who have not made it to the PGA Tour whom I will remember most: guys like Mark Lofye, Brian Bateman, Trip Kuehne and girls like Adele Moore, Jody Figley and Leslie Green.

Many people contributed to this project. The entire staff at the AJGA, especially Stephen Hamblin, Mark Stevens and Pete Ripa. Chris Haack at the University of Georgia, who during the writing of the book was able to win a national championship for the Bulldogs. A big thanks to South Carolina's Puggy Blackmon whose insight on junior and college golf provided depth. Jim Brown at Ohio State and Wally Goodwin at Stanford were also very generous. I am also appreciative to Mike Kelly at Nike Golf and the families of all the players, especially Nancy Leonard, Dr. Larry Leonard and Phil and Mary Mickelson, for allowing me to reflect on their personal stories.

Thanks to Roland Lazenby who both coached and inspired the work. And to Eric Trethewey at Hollins University who helped me uncover the true character of each player. Thanks to Jon Scott, Brad Faxon, Mike Biggs, Mac Barnhardt, Tom Watson, Alison Thietje, Randy Smith, Irv Batten, Jack Nicklaus, Scotty Cameron, Jeff Monday, Cliff Fischer, Norrie West, Ford Fischer, Trip Kuehne, Ernie Kuehne, Matt Kuchar, Brian Bateman, Harry Rudolph, Justin Leonard, Phil Mickelson, David Duval, Tiger Woods and Jim Furyk. And a special salute to Buck and JoAnn Levy in Sun Valley and Hank George in the Scotty Cameron/Titleist Putter Studio.

A special thanks to Harold Ramis and the movie *Caddyshack*.

Thanks to Tom Bast who directed the experience and to my associate editor, Kathleen Wingfield, for the final summer's journey.

I want to thank my family: Catherine, your voice and support made this possible. Your devotion is unending, and it pervades our family everyday. And to Ryan and Emma, never, ever stop dreaming.

Last but not least, I want to thank Glen Day. Your absence from the 1987 AJGA summer staff gave me an opportunity to meet hundreds of kids with smiles, loose swings and bucket hats.

The entire process of writing this book took more than two years. When I began, Bob Johnson was using a short Ping Anser putter, and when I finished he was using a 60-inch "chest-holder" model. Thanks also to Linda "Nina" Johnson who provided family support and an English teacher's direction. To Mark Scheerer and Mary Lee Bradford, I can only imagine what a beach trip will be without a laptop. And to my brother-in-law, Dave Linden, your swing is like Furyk's, but it's your short game I admire. And Lisa, tell Julie MacArthur that I want an interview.

More important than anything in this creation is knowing that some of the junior days will be handed to the next generation. I hope it humbles and inspires.

Thanks also to AJGA roadies Dan Aehl, Eric Nordlie and Scott Frisch. A special thanks to Scott and Suzi Hodoval. Hoots, thanks for showing me that I was better off writing about the sport. To Hank Kuehne, Matt Kuchar and Charles Warren: your games were not documented in this book, but I have a feeling that you will become masters of the millennium.

Lastly, there is one thing that I hope never changes—the bastion of innocence known as junior golf. It has a quality that teaches young people about so much more than golf.

INTRODUCTION

White Bucket Hats and Confidence

The mid-1970s was an exciting time in the world of golf. Jack Nicklaus, Tom Weiskopf and Johnny Miller battled head to head. Lee Elder was invited to play at Augusta, becoming the first black ever to tee it up at the Masters. Tom Watson appeared on the scene as a Nicklaus challenger and at the British Open in red plaid pants.

Golf apparel reached a flamboyant level of eyeball-popping colors. Pastels, plaids, stripes, wide white belts and sharp dagger-like collars were the rage. Hubert Green actually wore green polyester pants, and Nicklaus had a pair of bright yellow pastels. It was a vibrant time, and threads were plug-em in at night, glow-in-the-dark outrageous. This included headwear; white bucket hats and visors covered trendy hair styles. Sponsor names like Amana and big alligator logos that represented Izod adorned the headgear like billboards. Chi Chi Rodriguez's sword dance strut was better than any end-zone dance.

There was the birth of Eldrick Woods to Earl and Kultida and an inauspicious dinner at the Sea Turtle restaurant in Jacksonville, Florida. This was just a dinner meeting at a junior clinic. Tom Watson, Puggy Blackmon and Mike Bentley talking junior golf and eating stuffed flounder. Bentley was doing most of the talking; Watson and Blackmon listened intently. Bentley's agenda was to get Watson to be his honorary chairman for a new national junior golf association. Watson was just beginning to dominate on Tour, and Bentley saw him as a perfect fit for a national spokesperson for his new organization, which up to this point was just verbal hyperbole. Somehow, Bentley was going to create a national playground for junior golf, something similar to a PGA Tour, only for 11-18-year-old boys and girls. Everyone at dinner that night agreed it was a great idea.

Based in Atlanta, Bentley forged ahead with his plan. He changed the names on the junior program in Atlanta like a rotating title sponsor at a PGA event. In 1978 he ushered the Dekalb County Junior into the Atlanta Junior, and then before any 14-year-old could put a peg in the ground, the adoption of the moniker American Junior Golf Association (AJGA) became the dimpled cover exterior of the junior game. It was really the Dekalb County junior and the AJGA under one roof. Bentley saw both a need and an opportunity to create an overall structure to further foster the game on a competitive, amateur grassroots level. "I thought it was a great idea at the time, but I thought he would starve," said Blackmon. With that in mind, Blackmon turned his two Jacksonville junior events into a chapter of the national structure, giving Bentley a club length's support—humble beginnings. The AJGA still had little cash flow and it began running two Tournaments (the American Junior Classic and the Tournament of Champions). A member of the AJGA board of directors, Kay Slayden, created a first Tournament home for the Tournament of Champions at Inverrary in Lauderhill, Florida. Inverrary had been the longtime site of the PGA Tour's Jackie Gleason and the inital home of the PGA Tour Players Championship. The American Junior Classic was welcomed by the Innisbrook Golf Resort in Tarpon Springs, Florida. All of a sudden, Tournaments at Inverrary and Innisbrook gave credibility to the fledgling nonprofit organization.

The first two Tournaments created a small national stage for a handful of junior golfers. Future PGA Tour players like Willie Wood, Jodie Mudd, Andrew Magee, Mark Calcavecchia, Jim Gallagher Jr., Mark Brooks, Andy Dillard and Tommy Moore saw the AJGA as an opportunity to compete with the country's best. Their pictures still hang at AJGA headquarters near Atlanta. "I saw the way they set up one of the first Tournaments at Inverrary," recalls Blackmon. "I told them it was too difficult, the kids won't finish. Willie Wood went out and shot 66."

The AJGA was certainly not the first organization to initiate national Tournament golf for juniors. The USGA has organized the Boys' Junior Amateur event since 1948, when Dean Lind defeated Ken Venturi in Ann Arbor, Michigan. Events like the "Big I" Insurance Classic, the PGA Junior, the Optimist World and the Hudson Junior have all contributed to the development of junior golf. But, as far as a complete Tournament schedule is concerned, utilizing national sponsors and courses that test young minds and games, the AJGA was the beginning.

Like most great concepts, it started with Bentley's vision. But Bentley, the visionary of the future of junior golf, was caught in the middle of the program's structure. Chris Haack joined Bentley in 1981 to handle Tournament operations for both events so Bentley could raise funds. A year later the AJGA had a permanent headquarters at Horeshoe Bend Country Club in Roswell, Georgia. About this same time junior golf began to erupt just like Bentley's vision. Watson came on board as the national spokesperson. The AJGA's initial Tournament offerings escalated to six events. The junior players started to realize that there was somewhere else to compete. Blackmon said, "What happened was kids that were big fish in a little pond become the little fish in the big pond. All of a sudden, the ability to play at a higher level raised everyone's game."

Stephen Hamblin, a teaching pro at Innisbrook, took the reins from a distraught Bentley and became the organization's executive director in 1984. "That same year we almost closed the doors," said Hamblin. The AJGA had a board of directors in place but little working capital. They were lean years according to Hamblin. The AJGA persevered slowly, developing a cadre of efficiently organized and staffed Tournaments nationwide.

Today there are more than 4,500 members of the AJGA. Hamblin and his staff of 30 direct more than 50 Tournaments a year.

Blackmon was teaching his golf camp in South Carolina earlier this summer, when one of his campers asked about David Duval. "What was David Duval like as a junior?" asked one camper. In Blackmon's mind was a picture of an 18-year-old Duval wearing a white bucket hat, the kind with the brim that covers the periphery of the entire lid. Blackmon was unable to resist the urge to tell the story about Duval's freshman year at Georgia Tech. Like a lot of AJGA alumni, Duval was a maverick, plotting his own confident course. His last summer with the AJGA, Duval wore a white bucket at many junior events and at the beginning of his freshman year at Georgia Tech. Blackmon took a picture of Duval wearing shorts, white golf shoes and socks, a bucket hat and a bright pink shirt. Blackmon had the picture transferred to a mouse pad and sent it to the headquarters of Tommy Hilfiger Golf. Before the 1997 PGA Tour season, Duval went to Tommy Hilfiger Golf headquarters to be fitted for apparel. While at the office, he was reintroduced to the retro photo of his early college days. All Duval could think was, "Coach, I'm going to kill him."

Duval was not the only junior that wore a white bucket hat. In the late 1980s the white bucket hat for the boys' junior player was cool. "That's all I remember about Duval, that gosh-ugly white bucket hat he wore," said Haack. "And Leonard wore one of those hats, too. I can remember more than a dozen players wearing those things," said Haack. Trip Kuehne recalls that the bucket hat brigade started at La Paloma for the AJGA team championship. "It was so hot in the desert that we would fill those things with water and dump them over our head to cool off. It was also a great sun protector," said Kuehne.

Jack Nicklaus wore a white bucket hat to compete for most of the 1965 and 1966 PGA Tour seasons. He set a trend wearing the fashionable headgear, winning back-to-back (1965, 1966) Masters and one British Open (1966). The American 20-something players were not even born. Al Geiberger and Don January donned bucket hats in the 1970s. To Leonard and Duval, January was the first month of the year and Geiberger may as well have been a lunch special at the TPC Woodlands grill. To the junior golfers in the late 1980s, the white bucket hat was just another trend in bravado for the junior players with a game. *No Fear* t-shirts, *Air Jordans*, white bucket hats and roller blades, just another fad in the mix. It was an accessory that looked cool and kept them cool.

Another factor in the development of the current young players on the PGA Tour, was the ability to compete in the same arena with young ladies at the junior level. The AJGA was not a single-gender school with a gated entry. Jetting around the country to compete against Phil Mickelson, Jim Furyk and David Duval was incentive enough. But throw in Kelly Robbins, Vicki Goetze, Adele Moore, Christy Erb and Liza LaBelle competing on the same course. All of a sudden, the game's fascination was filled with one more distraction. Driving-range chatter was about more than just the day's score.

As the national junior game gathered momentum, college scholarships gave parents another reason for *junior* and *sissy* to pursue the sport. The AJGA and other junior Tournaments became an "investment." Could there be a quality return on the investment? Jetting to Tournaments in Tahoe, Denver, Palm Beach, Dallas and some remote areas like French Lick, Indiana, was costly. The economics of junior golf also limited the accessibility of the AJGA. Some families could simply not afford the exorbitant costs of travel.

At this time the NCAA was cutting back the number of scholarships afforded sports like football, and spring sports like golf benefited. At the NCAA Division I level, golf was being ruled by a small majority. Wake Forest, Houston, Texas, Florida, Ohio State and Oklahoma State dominated the competition. From 1962 to 1987, these six schools were college golf. Since the junior game gathered momentum (1988-1999), ten different schools have won the team title. Parity was quickly becoming the norm. "It was no longer a guessing game. More schools were able to locate the players and everyone benefited," said Blackmon. Mike Holder went from being the only college coach at AJGA events to one of more than a dozen of his contemporaries at select events. "When I was recruited to Oklahoma State, Mike Holder was easy to talk to because he was the only coach I remember seeing at the events. I knew exactly who

I was talking to, but that was not the case for some of the other schools," said Harry Rudolph.

AJGA results quickly became the most important piece of mail (now electronic mail) for college coaches like Rick LaRose (Arizona), Steve Loy (Arizona State) and Wally Goodwin (Stanford).

Older coaches like George Hannon (Texas) and Jesse Haddock (Wake Forest) had coached players like Longhorns Tom Kite, Ben Crenshaw and Deamon Deacons Lanny Wadkins and Curtis Strange. They recruited on the basis of their reputation. Being progressive in a changing game would soon be an issue athletic directors would have to meet head-on. College golf continues to be a sport where the individual egos and games are packaged incongruently. It is like fitting a watermelon in a ball washer. Never has such an individual game been twisted to make it a team event, and coaching the individual personality is more important than coaching the swing. Coaching during the Tournament is reduced to a rugby scrum of coaches meeting on the back-nine par threes to educate their players on what club to hit.

As the junior and college games began to find their stance, the late 1980s brought on a new challenge. The AJGA was still searching for avenues to raise funds. Chris Haack, then the foundation director, decided to host a one-day Pro-Junior Tournament at the AJGA's host course and site of the Tournament of Champions, Horeshoe Bend Country Club. They asked current PGA Tour-playing AJGA alums to come back and play in a single-day event consisting of six-somes, one pro, four amateurs and a junior. This would be a six-hour round of golf in the spirit of raising money for junior golf. Players such as Davis Love III, Brad Faxon, Sam Randolph, Willie Wood and Andrew Magee and LPGA player Kris Tschetter returned. The event was both a financial and public relations success. But, maybe more important was a call Love made to Chris Haack, the night before the outing. Love explained he would have to cancel, but he wanted to contribute to the junior program financially. Haack said, "I realized then that their time was maybe more important than anything. Their commitment to what we were doing was important, but not as important as the time they would take off to come in and play."

Following the event, Haack ran the idea of the PGA Tour players donating 1 percent of the annual earnings past then 20-something PGA Tour players Bob Tway and Willie Wood. The concept was simple. "This way they could help us out financially, and it hurt each player only incrementally based on the kind of year he would have,"said Haack. Haack and AJGA board member Allen Layland cooperated in structuring the framework, which is still in place today, generating thousands each year for the development of the program. Haack remembers Tway's initial response. "I hope I write you a check for $10,000 each year." Even players such as Peter Jacobsen, who did not play in AJGA events, signed up. The 1-percent club is the best club in the AJGA's bag of fund-raising.

However, the growth of the AJGA came with some growing pains. In the early days of the AJGA, getting in Tournaments was a tough ticket for the boys. The AJGA's most difficult task was objectively picking players for the Tournament field. Comparing résumés of junior players from remote areas of the country was tough to do from a single-page entry form. Picking the fields for some of the more popular events was wrought with comparing unknown local Tournament from places like Minot, North Dakota, and Manchester, Vermont. The system wasn't perfect and the parent phone calls came fast and furious. Some current PGA Tour players were not allowed to play in AJGA events because their résumé was not up to par. Since the problem exacerbated itself, the AJGA added qualifiers to filter the unknowns through a pre-Tournament qualifier. The odds to make a field through the AJGA qualifiers are sometimes brutal, but it has become the fair way to handle objections.

Phil Mickelson, Justin Leonard, David Duval and Tiger Woods played in AJGA events growing up. It was a small arena of their development as golfers. They learned the rules, experienced the competition and came to understand the decorum of the game. They were exposed to some of the nation's best courses, places like the TPC Woodlands, English Turn and La Paloma. And they took their games to obscure corners of the golfing world like the Flint Elks Lodge 222 in Flint, Michigan, and Otter Creek in Columbus, Indiana. The national junior scene was not part of their summer vacation from school; it *was* their summer vacation. Their Tournament schedules in some ways were more concentrated than they are today. They have arrived at golf's defining level with the physical game and instinct for success. They were able to demonstrate a passion and drive for the game. But, mostly they were able to have fun.

When Phil Mickelson returned home from a summer of junior Tournaments his parents made him go straight to the calculator. They would say, "Add up every dime you spent." The Mickelsons did not want their teenage son to repay them. They wanted him to realize he was spending "real" money.

When Justin Leonard became a player representative for the AJGA he was supposed to be an ambassador for the players, giving board members a way to understand the mind set of the typical junior golfer.

David Duval was told that he couldn't play in every junior event so he had to make choices based on economics. The game was not a summer free-for-all, it was a proving ground.

Earl and Kultida Woods pulled their son back several times and explained some of the barriers that exist in the game. The Charlie Siffords and the Lee Elders left the door slightly ajar, but there would be more than just golf that their son would have to deal with along the way to the PGA Tour.

Woods, Duval, Mickelson and Leonard realized early that the game was more than just a game. They also realized it afforded them a magnificent opportunity. Leonard was so affected by his junior days he now helps organize the annual AJGA Justin Leonard team event in Dallas. Mickelson contributes in a similar way. He hosts the Phil Mickelson Junior Championship, held on four courses in the San Diego area each summer. Duval's recent remarks about the Ryder Cup revenues was not so he could line his own pockets. He wanted some of the money to go to the Jacksonville area to help connect kids with the game in junior golf. And the Tiger Woods Foundation might be the best single pilot program that affords anyone with dreams and a swing a chance to play.

The AJGA starts with starters saying, "Play away, please," but between the innocent invitation and the 18th hole is a competitive skirmish. "I was friends with kids off the course, but on the course I wanted to beat their brains out," said Trip Kuehne. Typical AJGA Tournaments have kids from more than thirty different states represented. In the 1980s a kid from Mannheim, Pennsylvania, like Jim Furyk, met kids from Dallas like Justin Leonard, Cade Stone and Trip Kuehne. And kids from Houston like Tina Trimble got to know players from Delray Beach, Florida, like Michelle McGann. Not many other sports created a junior amateur landscape quite like this. It became a melting pot of swings, personalities and abilities. Mickleson would sit and watch the likes of Seve Ballesteros and say, "Someday I'm going to play like that. Someday I'm going to win that trophy."

There was a sense that this competition kindled a respect for the game which allowed him to test his game against the very best. Mickelson went so far as to wear long pants to play junior matches. Ninety-degree heat, and 16-year-old Phil Mickelson was playing the part of a professional golfer. Duval let his game talk one victory at a time. Woods did not just play junior golf, he lived junior golf. He carved a way to dominate, digesting each player he played with, each course he played on and came to understand the nuances along the way. Leonard, Duval, Woods and

Mickelson are proving to the world that golf is a game that can never be mastered, but they are going to push their abilities to the limit. They are the *masters of the millennium*. Their vision to excel beyond their own expectations makes them hungry in a sport that only rewards one thing—success. Seven-figure endorsement deals make it easy to put the tee in the ground, but knowing that the small, dimpled sphere must travel 7,000 yards with a purpose makes it a little tougher to draw the club back.

The mastery of the game has become one of the toughest skills in sports today. Hitting a Randy Johnson fastball, returning a Pete Sampras serve and beating Dominic Hasek gloveside tests skill. But, for a minute, forget titanium shafts, super-charged golf balls and turf equipment. The 20th century closes with a drum roll. The last part of the decade has been a parade of young players staking claim to the notion that the torch is being passed from players like Nicklaus and Watson to the next capable generation.

Time has ticked away decades, years, months, days, hours and minutes.

Since the very beginning in 1934, when Sam Snead turned professional at the age of 22 and when Horton Smith, at the ripe age of 25, won the first Masters. That same year, Paul Runyan was crowned the first leading money winner on the PGA Tour. His take was $6,767, but a statement issued by the PGA in its very first year of existence may have had a more profound impact. These were the days of the depression, the most economically critical days the nation had ever endured, and in February, the PGA asked that golf professionals give free lessons to children to help popularize the game. The idea was to get the kids involved so they could mature with the game.

The '30s was a grand decade. Gene Sarazen's double eagle on 15 won the Masters in 1935, and the youngster Smith returned the favor the next year. They were the "kids" back then, with nicknames just like today's players. There was "Sir Walter" (Walter Hagen) and "the Squire" (Gene Sarazen). Bobby Jones, Frances Ouimet, Snead and Ben Hogan are now simply legends.

As the game enters the new millennium, there is another marked change. A game which builds bridges, built firmly on tradition, is celebrating a renaissance of the younger player. The next generation of the PGA Tour has the equipment like no generation before. These new golfing greats have empowered their will to succeed just like the young players who came generations before them. The names on the leader boards are changing with each passing Tournament. Instead of Watson, Miller, Nicklaus and Floyd, names like Mickelson, Woods, Leonard, Els, Duval,

Furyk and Westwood are appearing with regularity. Snead was honest at the 1997 Masters when he predicted Tiger Woods would "be great in three or four years." Instead, it was the year he Toured the dogwoods in record-breaking style.

Woods, Leonard and Mickelson made their way from the junior game to the Crow's Nest at Augusta National. Duval went from king of the national junior scene to being named an All-American four straight years. His game developed thanks to a perpetuation of consistency. Each player went from the proving ground of junior golf to America's playground with conviction, and it all really happened in less than two decades. Mickelson has played in three Ryder Cups, Leonard two, Woods two and Duval, incredibly, just one. Will the new millennium mark the continued rise of this foursome at golf's defining level? Or will the crowd behind them surpass their hungry eyes?

Reflecting on a game is a difficult thing to do when the future is so promising.

In the mid-'80s, even golf ball companies developed a relationship with the AJGA. Enter a Tournament and get a dozen balls. The AJGA vans would load up their staff, hitch the trunk (nicknamed Ellie) to the van and travel down the road to the next Tournament. Packed deep inside Ellie were thousands of Titleists. How many of these juniors would grow up hitting the golf ball with the Titleist label? Titleist CEO Wally Uihlein makes sure his company is involved with generations of players. The actual dollar signs, commas and zeroes involved in Leonard, Duval, Mickelson or Woods' deals are not public knowledge. Their agents are not quick to "divulge the deals." In 1989, Titleist became the AJGA presenting sponsor. "They really don't make a big deal out of it," said Hamblin. "They just like being involved." It is amazing what a dozen golf balls do to the visage of a 15-year-old. Assistant executive director Pete Ripa said, "At each event we give them so many options (varieties of golf balls), it's like choosing a color of a Ferrari."

For this foursome, junior golf was an innocent playground where they developed as individuals and players. Duval's hottest summer for scoring was in 1989. At the AJGA event at English Turn, Duval shot 73 the hard way. He went out in 40 and brought it home in 33. In his group that day was Brian Bateman, who said, "He showed me something. A lot of guys would pack it in. He never gave up and he hasn't stopped." Typical junior players can't turn the tide like this foursome. And now they are spinning their tricks on the PGA Tour at the expense of some qualified veterans. Davis Love III knows it, Brad Faxon knows it; so do Tom Lehman and Greg Norman. How much more does it take before week after week the winner is "whatchamacallit, one of those young turks, hits it a mile, putts the eyeballs out of it, you know."

In 1999, Phil Mickelson almost met destiny at the U.S. Open at Pinehurst, Justin Leonard came oh-so-close to kissing the claret jug, again. David Duval had one sleeve in the green jacket in 1998 before Mark O'Meara decided to win one for the older guys. And Tiger Woods won his second major for the ages at Medinah.

Payne Stewart told Mickelson, "You'll get yours." Paul Lawrie said to Leonard, "You've already had yours." The golf demons have said to Duval, "You'll appreciate yours now that you have come close to tasting the nectar." And Woods may have arrived back from the woods, where he learned that distance is for long driving contests and that the real fun is in the short game.

This isn't the future of professional golf. This is professional golf. The tide is starting to roll back in and the waves are about to pound the surf. What an awe-inspiring foursome. Jacksonville, Dallas, San Diego and Orlando. A mature left-hander with a Mickelsonian innocence; an organized tactician (Leonardo the great); a cerebral, plodding birdie machine (Groovy Duuvy) and a harnessed set of expectations, skills and emotions (Tiger Woods). What do these guys all have in common off the course? Very little. What do they share on the course? The rare ability to score. Forget sand saves, greens in regulation and that they were the youngest and fastest American foursome to earn a million bucks. These guys flat-out put the ball in the hole in fewer strokes than their contemporaries.

As the new millennium dawns, these four lead a pack of young players on Tour who have attitude and a decided experience fostered in the ability to play in professional events as amateurs. The game of professional golf doesn't just bridge generations, it provides a wide, green fairway for young men to hone their game better than any other sport on the globe. It coddles and nurtures the youth like a sport that wants to build on its benchmark. It all started with kids yanking at their father's leg, saying, "Dad, I want to play in that." Junior golf is a bastion of innocence and etiquette wrapped tightly around tradition. It's about kids with smiles and loose swings. Some of them wear white bucket hats.

JUST IN TIME

Nancy Leonard looked over in the passenger's seat. Justin's arms were cradled around the winner's trophy for the American Junior Golf Association (AJGA) Oklahoma Junior Classic, held just outside of Tulsa at Indian Springs Golf Club in Broken Arrow, Oklahoma. After 36 holes, Leonard was tied with Robert Boisvert, from Edmond, Oklahoma, at 150. Leonard made par on the first playoff hole to edge Boisvert and win his first national junior title. She was looking for an exit where she could stop and call home and Royal Oaks Country Club to let everyone know about the 13-year-old champion from Dallas, her son. With Justin asleep, she was left to review the Tournament with the chatty junior in the backseat, Harrison Frazar. Frazar had also competed in the Tournament and would later be Leonard's freshman roommate and teammate at the University of Texas. He would also join Leonard on the PGA Tour in 1998.

When Leonard finally woke up the next day, his mom was his transportation to Royal Oaks, a short trip from the Leonard home in Lake Highlands. Randy Smith, Leonard's golf instructor teacher since 1977, was teaching a lesson on the range when

Leonard approached, hoisting the trophy into the Dallas sky. "When Justin showed up with the trophy," Smith hesitated as he remembered the junior version of Leonard, "that put a little heat on old Randall," Smith added pointing to his heart. Smith said Leonard's win in Oklahoma made him realize Leonard was capable of "big things on the golf course."

10:52 A.M., JUNE 10, 1987

Meridian Golf Club in Englewood, Colorado, is a classic British links-style course. Designed by Jack Nicklaus, the course typifies a respect for the unrestrained natural setting, that is the signature of so many British and Scottish courses. If it weren't for the impeding view of the downtown Denver skyline and the business development center encircling the course, the mind's eye could escape to the land where golf is played in its purest form.

On this bright summer morning, bag-toting junior golfers were everywhere. The typical putting green chatter and coffee-sipping parents dotted the practice area around the clubhouse. The American Junior Golf Association (AJGA), the equivalent of the PGA Tour for juniors, was sending eleven eighteen-year-old boys and girls out on the course with precision. AJGA executive director Stephen Hamblin did not make a habit of announcing the first tee, but on this day, the second round of the Meridian Western Junior Classic, his enthusiasm was supposed to set an example for the young staff.

Announcements for tee times were made with handheld megaphones. Like Titleists flying into the thin air of the mile-high city, the sound was far reaching. Hamblin's voice echoed above the background chatter. "Leonard, Justin Leonard, please report to the first tee." Hamblin's eyes searched the putting area for any movement, but he saw nothing. At 10:55, Hamblin checked his watch and distributed scorecards to the two nervous 14-year-olds. As he went over the course rules and post-round instructions, he glanced one more time for the missing player, Justin Leonard, from Dallas, Texas. Nothing.

Considering the waiting list to enter Tournaments, qualifying events held to solidify the field, and the exorbitant cost for junior players to jet around the country and compete against the best juniors in America, missing a tee time was something Hamblin or his staff rarely needed to address.

Hamblin simplified USGA and local rules for the departing twosome. "Your third, Mr. Leonard, has five minutes to catch you; at that point, he's hitting three. If he doesn't hit it in five minutes and you guys finish one, you are playing alone. He's DQ'd. Play well." Once the two players hit their tee shots, Hamblin added, "If he catches you, you will redistribute cards after the first hole."

Hamblin started the five-minute time period with few expectations. The small clubhouse at Meridian sits on a knoll, and the small parking lot is visible from the first tee. At this point, Hamblin's eyes zeroed in on the parking lot. Because of the office park setting, cyclists used the perimeter of the golf course as a criterium-like training area. A pack of about twenty cyclists were part of the peripheral activity around the golf course. Hamblin thought if Leonard was going to show, he would be hunched over like a cyclist, bearing down on the first tee.

As Hamblin's watch approached the four-minute mark, a car screeched into the Meridian parking lot. By this time the news that Leonard was on the watch had made its way to the entire group of parents and players still waiting to tee off. In silence, the fourteen-year-old Leonard slid out of the car, grabbed his bag, tugged on his spikes and made it to the first tee, just in time.

Dr. Larry Leonard's car exceeded the posted 25-mile-per-hour speed limit signs of the planned business community, so he and Justin knew it was going to be close. Leonard's dad, Larry, who brought Justin to Denver, was visiting a lab on business when he got a call from his son. "My alarm didn't go off, and I just missed the course shuttle; my tee time is in twenty minutes," yelled Justin. Even at the age of fourteen, Leonard knew missing a tee time was not the first impression he wanted to portray to the AJGA.

When he arrived, Hamblin smiled and said, "Glad you could make it, Mr. Leonard. You're hitting three." Then Hamblin added the heat, "And if you aren't able to catch the players before they finish the hole, you are disqualified."

Leonard remembers the word "disqualified" vividly. That was the impetus for the tardy youngster to start waving at the two players on the green as if to say, "I'm here." Brian Bateman was one of the players on the first green. He had just marked his four-foot par putt when he noticed Leonard. "I looked back and I saw Justin waving his arms like a madman," said Bateman. Bateman put his ball back down and took away his mark and re-thought his routine: "If I roll this four-footer in, he's disqualified." Bateman re-marked and watched the first tee.

The 401-yard first hole is a straightaway par four with fairway bunkers down the right side. Without a practice swing, Leonard hit his third shot of the day into the Denver air; it landed safely. He grabbed his bag and broke into a half shuffle-run down the fairway. He quickly hit his second shot on the green and acknowledged Bateman's patience.

Leonard maneuvered through the 6,432-yard gorse-heather-lined fairways of Meridian in a six-over-par 78. This included two strokes on top for "my alarm clock," said Leonard. He added, "My friend had an earlier tee-time and I forgot to reset the alarm."

This was the last time Leonard, an admitted "meticulous" planner, ever missed a tee time. He looks back on his missed tee time and shrugged, "I was just happy to make it to the course."

Back in Dallas later that week, Nancy Leonard headed to a discount store. "I sat in the clock section of this store listening to the different alarms. I wanted the loudest alarm available," she said.

A few weeks later, Leonard was at a Tournament with Trip Kuehne, now famous for losing to Tiger Woods in the 1994 U.S. Amateur at TPC Sawgrass. As the morning alarm clock went off, Kuehne said, "That is the loudest alarm clock I've ever heard."

"There's a reason for that," said Leonard.

5:37 P.M., JUNE 8, 1997

Almost ten years to the day of Leonard's missed tee time, it was the ironic misfortune of another player, Mark Weibe, from Denver, which sent Leonard on a golfing summer like no other.

Weibe stood over a two-foot putt to ensure a playoff with Justin Leonard at the Kemper Open on the TPC at Avenel, just outside of Baltimore and the nation's capital. Weibe started the day three strokes ahead of Mike Springer, his nearest competitor, and five strokes ahead of Leonard. He three-putted 17, and like most Sunday back nines, the intensity of the last few holes was etched in Weibe's face. His sliding two-footer was sent on its way, and it narrowly missed the four-and-a-half-inch hole in the earth. Leonard watched greenside, as he suddenly became the 1997 Kemper Open champion. Weibe, who fought the effects of allergy medicine and a winless streak since the Hardee's Golf Classic (1986), had to bite the biscuit and settle for second place.

"I really would rather have seen him make the putt and us go into a playoff," said Leonard. He claimed his second win ever on Tour and his biggest paycheck to date, $270,000. The win catapulted Leonard to nineteenth on the Tour money list, and the alarm had finally sounded for the 24-year-old. He added, "Being able to go out and make some putts and put some pressure on the leader (Weibe) when nobody had really been able to do that all day long—I certainly thought about that Saturday night."

Leonard's low, closing-round 67 was enough to beat Weibe and three decent foreign players named Nick Faldo, Greg Norman and Nick Price, all of whom finished tied for third at 273. Price and Norman matched Leonard's 67 on Sunday, but both were too far back on Sunday to make a serious move. What Leonard did not know at the time was that his five-stroke come-from-behind winning margin would be the largest margin of the 1997 season. "It was absolutely a turning point for me," said Leonard.

The Kemper served as a warm-up for what many on Tour consider the biggest event of the year, the U.S. Open, two miles down the road at Congressional in Bethesda, Maryland.

10:52 A.M., JUNE 10, 1997

On the eve of the U.S. Open, Leonard's 25th birthday coming on, the day of the final round, his second win on Tour attached to his bag tag, the timing seemed right for his first major win. His mistake at Meridian was a distant memory. Leonard was busy preparing his presidential game for the long Congressional Country Club layout. As the rough was growing deeper and deeper in Bethesda because of Maryland rain showers, Leonard's major expectations were heightened when he Toured the 7,004-yard course in 69 on Thursday. He was just where a strong come-from-behind player should be at the U.S. Open Championship, four stokes behind Colin Montgomerie's opening 65. Leonard followed it up with a two-over-par 72 and at one over would make the cut easily. However, his third round, a 78, proved to be his undoing. He spiraled, due partly to the now-rainy conditions, which left the shorter-hitting Leonard with long irons in his hands for approach shots.

The USGA's patchwork efforts, because of players being left on the course due to lightning and rain, made the Open a quagmire of disarray. With order gone, Leonard's first major would have to wait. On Sunday, his 25th-birthday round was a blow-out-the-candles, even-par 70, which left him tied for 36th. After tying for seventh at Augusta in April, Leonard had to confront disappointment in his second major of the year.

3:30 P.M., JULY 20, 1997

Randy Smith's cellular phone usually rings on Sunday, some-time after the final round. This Sunday the call came from the 1997 British Open champion.

"What have I done?," said Leonard, calling just after escaping from his Marine hotel room and downing a pizza on the 17th green at Royal Troon with his caddy Bob Riefke. What Leonard had done was come from five strokes back, just as he had done at the Kemper, and stunned Jesper Parnevik and the rest of the field at the 1997 British Open. Leonard had claimed his first major.

Leonard requires order for success, and the order with which he finished the Tournaments leading up to the British was telling. He tied for fifth at the Fed Ex St. Jude Classic, and at the Motorola Western Open, he shot a second-round 64 and finished tied for third. The trend in his finishes, coupled with the way he approached the British, all added up—tied for fifth, tied for third. Pass the scones and put the iced tea in the claret jug. British Open champion.

Leonard's Sunday front-nine 31 had been like an opening act to the Dickens classic, *Oliver Twist*. With Smith at home and Leonard's parents also back in Dallas, he was an orphan from Texas. Leonard birdied two, three, and four, and quizzically said, "May I have more, please." Leonard, who respected the British Open championship enough to come over and qualify twice, got more when he birdied six, seven and nine. Offset with a bogey at five and a par at the famous and aptly named Postage Stamp eighth, Leonard went out in 31, and he stamped his own message on the leader board that he was a contender.

"There is a certain comfort coming from behind that I enjoy," said the long-shot Longhorn from Texas.

At this point, Leonard trailed Jesper Parnevik by two shots, but Leonard always liked being the underdog. Junior golf parents and players would hint, "Kid's got a great game, but he can't hit it far enough to play at the next level." It motivated the junior golfer. Then, at the University of Texas, Leonard grabbed ahold of something he learned from two alumni, Tom Kite and Ben Crenshaw: "Find a way to get the ball in the hole."

He practiced until Randy Smith kicked him off the range and out of the sand traps at Royal Oaks, and now he was 18 holes from a major. The combatants were Parnevik, clad in purple pants for the final round, with his normal headgear—his hat skewed upward like he was donning a rally cap in the Wrigley Field bullpen—and little Leonard, stoic and dapper—just a "kid" from Texas. It was Parnevik, the father of two girls named Peg (for a tee) and Pebble Peach (you guessed it), against the single guy.

The front nine typically plays downwind along the Firth of Clyde at Royal Troon. With the length of the back nine par fours, along with the windy conditions, the game suddenly changes at hole 10. It's argued that only wind and rain sculpt the terrain at Troon. The shorter-hitting Leonard did not pay much attention to the yardages. Instead, his instincts took over. The seaside links motto, *as much by skill as by strength,* personified Leonard's physical and mental approach to the back nine.

PGA Tour statistics distinguished the gorse-laden meadow grass and dunes that skirt the back nine as the toughest nine holes on Tour in 1997. Based on scoring average, 10 (3), 11(1), 15 (8) and 13 (10) were among the ten toughest golf holes. The statistics make it look as though the British cup-cutter forgot to cut a hole in the 11th green during his morning duties. A combined 39 double bogeys and 22 triple bogeys were marked on scorecards of the world's best players in the British Championship. In his first round, Tiger Woods earned one of the triple bogeys at 10, and then in his second round, he battled a tall gorse bush at the 11th before succumbing and taking a quadruple bogey eight.

Leonard's victory journey began at 10 where the 5-foot-9 Texan made bogey. Leonard said, "My chip at 10 was the difference. I really hit a poor chip, and I was about twenty feet from the hole. I missed my putt and had to swallow a bogey." Smith watched the bogey at 10 unfold from his dimly lit living room back in Dallas. "That was the defining moment," said Smith. He added, "There was a look about Justin. I've seen it several times. It was a look of O.K. Interesting, no harm, no foul, I'm comfortable and at peace with the world. I'm going to the 11th." Smith paints a verbal picture of spontaneous combustion at 11. Royal Troon's course literature offers a vivid description of the tee shot at 11. It says, "Imagine standing on a mountaintop and gazing over a rainforest canopy; that's the tee shot at the 463-yard eleventh."

Smith said, "I think the bogey at 10 just woke him up a little. His tee shot at 11 was straight to the house."

Parnevik was the only player in the field to beat par (35) on the back nine all three days prior. Par, as it often is at major championships, turned out to be the defining standard at Troon. Leonard said, "I think I am a better player when par is a good score and the course puts a premium on all parts of the game." Leonard thinks the mental scale is also tilted in majors. "Because par is the standard, it makes the mental game that much more important. Majors make me excel at my game. Partly because of my limitations physically," added Leonard. Once he scrambled for par at the 11th, Leonard reeled off four straight pars, while Parnevik was beginning to falter.

The week before Leonard headed to Scotland, Smith had made the diminutive Texan hit long irons, low shots, and bump-and-runs at Royal Oaks. "I even chipped balls off of the green, because some of the grass over there is tight," said Leonard. These shots were part of Smith's game plan to make Leonard's game suit Troon's uninhibited and windy setting. Growing up at Royal Oaks, Smith often instructed the junior Leonard to trim tree branches with wedges to improve his accuracy. With the number of trees lining the Royal Oaks practice area, this game has also been applied to a revolving group of juniors on the practice range at Royal Oaks. Smith continues to utilize Leonard's targets as natural icons of inspiration in his teaching setting. "Justin's trimmed a lot of branches around here," said Smith.

At 15, he needed the chip of his lifetime. Showing his calm, he picked up an empty beer cup and pretended to take a break and have some ale. His shot nestled to within 12 feet of the cup. Leonard's putt dropped dead center for par, and he showed an uncharacteristic display of emotion.

Was this starting to be fun? Leonard smiled and admitted, "That was the Tournament right there."

With all the length and little margin for error that Troon offers tee to green, it was Leonard's specially built Scotty Cameron putter that was the difference on the 17th hole, where Leonard would also have his post-Tournament meal. Leonard eyed his 35-foot putt with Riefke on the par 3. "I wasn't thinking about birdying the hole. But I knew the putt was going in about two feet from the hole," said Leonard.

The game's oldest golf championship was starting to tilt in Leonard's direction. Now 6-under for the day, 12-under for the championship, Leonard heard a groan from the 16th green as he was walking to the 18th tee. "I figured that was Jesper missing a putt." Sure enough, Parnevik missed a birdie opportunity at 16, which proved to be his undoing.

Leonard hit a blind tee shot to a few yards from fairway bunkers on 18. He then split the green and two-putted for par. The British Open championship, and its symbol, the claret jug, were in the hands of what the British press called "the little Texan with the flat swing." Leonard would exchange with the press all week to the effect that "If you were 5-9, 165 pounds, and had a size 10-C shoe, you would swing that way, too."

The Open championship at Troon had been Americanized in 1962 when Arnold Palmer won the inaugural classic. Tom Weiskopf found glory in 1973, and another Tom—Watson—emerged as the champion in 1982 after Troon was elevated to regal status and known as Royal Troon. Then came Mark Calcavecchia's playoff win over Wayne Grady and Greg Norman in 1989. From Daly (1995) to Tom Lehman (1996) and now Leonard, the U.S. had won the last three British Opens.

Leonard shrugs aside the notion his win was in any way Dickensian. "I did study Brit Lit at Texas, but it didn't take. I was not really a great English student. I was more math."

After Leonard added up his math, 65 strokes, he started last-minute preparations for something he hadn't planned, a little English. While English wasn't his strength, his dad had taught him a form of English, list making. Leonard credits his post-round list for what proved to be an eloquent acceptance speech. "I just made some notes; it's kind of second nature to me," said Leonard.

Leonard's sister Kelly talks about her dad's organization: "My dad makes lists for everything. I remember when I graduated from Texas, his little method of organization with 3 x 5 note cards. I did it for a while and then I developed my own method. Justin has his own method." Kelly added, "The lists help to get the results we want."

A microbiologist, Dr. Larry Leonard takes a scientific approach to his vocation, and a little has rubbed off on his kids. Leonard still makes lists. "I actually like to make lists so that everything is recorded. It's pretty much through the whole season. Randy also has a copy of the lists," said Leonard.

The claret jug hadn't yet hit the tarmac of Dallas-Fort Worth Airport, but the feeling of triumph had already hit Royal Oaks. "I had some damage in the pro shop; they were screaming in the Garden Room. In many ways, Royal Oaks has been a home away from home," said Smith.

Leonard wanted badly to be at Royal Oaks to celebrate with Smith and his family. His visualization of his proud family and the guys at Royal Oaks made his speech at Royal Troon hard to complete.

There was another reason he missed the states; this one was based on appetite. "Royal Oaks makes the best bacon cheeseburger in the world," said Leonard.

Congratulations starting pouring in for Leonard like champagne from the jug. Tom Kite, the 1997 Ryder Cup captain and one of Leonard's childhood role models, was one of the first to congratulate him on his victory, "Welcome to the team." Kite and Ben Crenshaw had been mentors to Leonard. They shared Texas as their alma mater, along with NCAA championships twenty years apart.

One of the items on Leonard's 1997 list was to be in Spain, with the Ryder Cup team, in September at Valderrama. With his British Open win, Leonard was assured of reaching his goal.

When Justin's plane finally landed in Dallas, his sister took in the moment as if it happened in slow motion. "As Justin walked into a private room where we had been waiting, my dad was the first to greet him. Justin handed the claret jug to my father— that's still my favorite picture, and I have it in our home."

So many thoughts invaded Smith as he watched the Open in the late morning hours from his darkened house. "It was if I was walking beside him the whole day, I knew how his mind was reeling and the emotion was too much." Smith acknowledged, "But, I don't think I will ever miss another British Open." Smith now often travels to the majors with Justin.

Smith points to Leonard's mental state as the reason for his British win. "Justin's just not intimidated. Does he thrive on it? Yes. Bigger galleries, yes. More exposure, yes. The bigger the stage, the more tuned up."

At 20, when Leonard beat Tom Scherrer 8 & 7 to win the 1992 U.S. Amateur title at Muirfield, just outside of Columbus in Dublin, Ohio, he realized he would follow tradition and play the first two rounds at the Masters with another Texan, from Plano, Fred Couples. Couples won the green jacket in April.

Leonard's first Masters experience in 1993 was an awakening. The University of Texas junior marveled at Couples' demeanor and encouraging remarks.

"The 1993 Masters was special. It didn't matter if I tapped in from 18 inches or holed a ten-footer, Fred was encouraging," said Leonard. Smith remembers visiting Leonard on the range after his first round at Augusta. "I said, what did you learn from Freddy?" Smith added, "To Justin, what seemed like such a small thing, being gracious, was such a huge deal. Isn't it kind of ironic with what happened at the British?" laughed Smith.

On the final day of the British, it was again Couples paired with Leonard. Leonard's eyes got big, and he said, "You get a sense he's out there pulling for you, even though he has his own game." And as the back nine unfolded, it was Couples who put an exclamation point on the win. "The guy made 140 feet of putts out there."

Leonard didn't make a list to play with Couples in the British, but he claims it was by design. "On 17 (Saturday), I said, let's go ahead and make this putt so we can play with Freddy tomorrow."

Since Leonard first handed the claret jug to his father after the British Open, it remained at his parents' house for safekeeping. "We moved it from room to room, depending on the occasion and how we wanted it displayed," said Nancy Leonard. The claret jug Toured the Leonard house much the way Justin Toured Royal Troon, with distinction and class. Nancy Leonard added, "And there has been a little champagne in the claret jug."

4:46 P.M., AUGUST 16, 1997

One month later, at the final major of the year, the PGA, Leonard again managed to climb into contention, this time on Saturday with a Winged Foot Country Club course-record 65. Leonard was quickly earning a reputation on Tour as a Thursday-Friday "hanger-on" and a Saturday-Sunday "contender." With Tom Kite and Lee Janzen seven strokes back, Leonard and Davis Love III would battle in what turned into a match-play event on Sunday. Leonard struggled in the middle of the round to find the fairway, while Love made a surge. On 13, with Love ahead by three strokes, the grinder from Texas thought he had an opportunity.

"I hit a good three iron to eight feet, Davis pulled a four-iron left of the green and had a real difficult shot without much green to work with." Love ended up chipping the ball, hitting the pin and having the ball come to rest two feet away from the cup. Leonard missed his birdie opportunity. "Davis told me later he had a decent lie on the chip. That was a situation where he looked like he was going to make bogey. I had a chance at birdie, but we both come away with pars."

After coming from five strokes back at the British, was Leonard too high on the leader board at the start of play on Sunday? Leonard casts aside this notion. "I just had a little trouble keeping the driver in the fairway during the middle of the round," He said. And as Love and Leonard walked up to the 18th green with the rainbow on the horizon, Leonard congratulated Love on his first major. "I told him that he should enjoy the moment, and I was proud of him," said Leonard. Love was more abrupt explaining the final steps up the 72nd hole. "I told Justin he was coming with me. I can't make it." From his acceptance speech at Troon to the class he showed as runner-up in the PGA, Leonard was quickly becoming one to watch in golf's big four.

Leonard's mind is always zeroed in on majors. He has an obvious respect for a certain Tournament in Georgia. "I'm very comfortable at Augusta. It's a huge mental battle that week because the placement of the balls on the green is so crucial, and I enjoy that. Having some success there, is something I look forward to," said Leonard. Leonard also added that the rest of the field will also be prepared. "Because of the seven- or eight-month break between majors, everybody is keyed up at the Masters. There is just a certain tradition that builds year after year."

In 1997, Love's PGA win made him the elder statesman of the 1997 major's quartet. Masters champion Tiger Woods (21), U.S. Open victor Ernie Els (27) and Leonard (25) were toddlers compared to Love. Leonard's record in the 1997 majors also strikes a preparatory pose. A top ten at the Masters, tied for 36th (U.S. Open), hoist the claret jug (British champion) and follow Love's soft spikes in second place at Winged Foot (PGA). Not bad for a 25-year-old from Dallas.

It is serendipitous to juxtapose Leonard's summer of 1987 with his summer of 1997. The Nicklaus Scottish-links course where he missed his tee time (1987) would prove to be similar in style to Royal Troon (1997). Nicklaus's design work and Leonard's golfing success met head-on several more times. At LaPaloma, another Nicklaus design, Leonard teamed with Trip Kuehne to win two AJGA Team Championships in 1989 and 1990. He won his U.S. Amateur title at Muirfield Village, considered in some ways Nicklaus's backyard, since he hosts the annual Memorial Tournament at the site. To compare the swing of each would be unfair, but the similarities go one step further. Leonard and Nicklaus are the only two players in the game to capture the NCAA championship, the U.S. Amateur and the British Open. Nicklaus grabbed his NCAA championship in 1959 and won the national amateur title in 1961. Leonard followed the two-year plan in 1992 and 1994. Leonard might not have the physical ability that Nicklaus used to his advantage, but they both rely on a keen sense of course management. Leonard's mind is unquestionably the extra club in his bag.

Ernie Kuehne, father to a pretty decent trio of amateur players named Trip, Kelli and Hank, observed Leonard as an eight-year-old battling his son Trip and then parsed his development against the world's best in modern times. "Justin Leonard will never win an athletic contest at anything, but you can't judge what's in a man's heart or more importantly, what's in his head, he said. "Leonard refuses to be denied. His will is beyond comparison in anything."

Leonard's real reputation on Tour is that of a "meticulous" planner. "With the schedules we keep, I just like to stay organized," said Leonard. Tour veteran Brad Faxon said, "His focus is that he is going to be the best player he can be. He's very organized, whether it be conditioning, working with his teacher or the amount of sleep he gets. He's (Tom) Kite-like. Nothing fancy, but he's got a great head."

There is also respect for the game which Leonard personifies. Twice (1993 and 1995) he traveled to the British in order to qualify. No one person sat Leonard down and said, "You need to revere this game." He assimilated the tradition of the game. Nike Tour veteran Harry Rudolph explained the junior version of Leonard as "the kind of kid you'd expect from the Dallas area who knew the tradition of the game and was always in control. There was something about his game, though. You'd keep his scorecard and at the end of the round, you just could not believe he was around par. You'd have to add it up three times and it just did not figure."

Leonard's reverence for the game was not really the reason he was one of the last PGA players to switch from a persimmon driver to metal.

"Justin always had the lead in changes," said Smith. "I never made it an issue, but I wanted him to hit metal."

In 1997, a few months before the British, Justin acknowledged that it was time.

Smith set out 14 or 15 drivers the week before the Texas swing on Tour. Leonard wanted to be able to control the trajectory of his tee shots, and he wasn't sure the metal would afford him the feel that he was getting from the persimmon.

Smith, forever the teacher with rules, did not allow Leonard to hit any kind of drive without a target. So, Smith's brother, with the gentle nudging of Smith, graciously offered to drive a cart 250 yards from where Leonard was swinging. Leonard grabbed the first driver, and after picking out his new target, he let the metal driver loose. As he sent his first ball airborne, Smith conceded he thought the ball was right on target. "I remember looking at the first couple and thinking, this stuff is good," said Smith. Leonard kept sending the tee balls out like bullets in a pattern. On about the eighth tee ball, Leonard swatted into orbit, Smith and Leonard stood admiring the flight. It was right on his target, the Royal Oaks golf cart positioned so that it was staring back at the range. The Leonard tee ball was so accurate, it knocked the windshield right out of the golf cart where his brother was now hunched on the floor for cover. "I had to order a new windshield for that cart, but it was worth it," said Smith.

5:43 P.M., MARCH 29, 1998

Walking up the 18th fairway at the 1998 Players' Championship, Leonard flashed a big smile and the Texas Longhorn, hook 'em horns symbol instead of the traditional victory "V". He had thought about the acknowledgment after his win at the British, but in retrospect, the British was a whirlwind of emotions in a short period of time.

In eerie similarity to the 1997 British and the Kemper Tournaments, Leonard started the final round five shots off the lead. He rolled a ten-footer in for eagle on 2 and then rallied for five birdies in seven holes beginning on 9. After his 9-iron on 17 (the infamous island green par three) found land, he displayed a rare sigh of relief and a roll of the eyes as if to say, I think I can handle it from here. "I am more comfortable with being in contention, and I think that just comes with experience," said Leonard. After erasing five stroke deficits at the Kemper, British and Tournament Players Championship, five might just be a magical number. No need for a lottery ticket, though; his 67 Sunday and four-day total (278) earned him the biggest payday on Tour in 1998, $720,000.

With the British Open, the Tournament Players Championship and the U.S. Amateur title, Leonard has added more than depth to the twenty-something crowd on Tour. The TPC also had another familiar Leonard theme—a foil. There was Mark Weibe at the Kemper, Jesper Parnevik at the British and Len Mattiace at the TPC.

The forever learned Leonard knows a little about taking heed of a bad experience. He shot 78 in the last round of the Tournament Players Championship in 1997. His 67 in 1998 was redemption, and he admits one of the items on his 1998 list was to improve his finish at the Tournament Players Championship.

As it happened at the British with his craving for a Royal Oaks cheeseburger, Leonard's Players Championship post-victory thoughts turned to his appetite. "Part of the reason we like it is because of the Thursday buffet in the locker room," he said.

One of the few in the 125-player field to enjoy a buffet on the Pete-Dye stadium course, Leonard followed the lead of a hot putter on Sunday. The conditions, hot and dry, were just how Leonard likes his course cooking. "Even in his amateur career, he would get hot as the weather got hotter," said Smith. "July, August, September, he has played some phenomenal golf." Leonard likes to think the weather is secondary. "I think it has more to do with the courses we typically play on Tour during those months."

Returning to the Tournament Players Championship in 1999, Leonard had to call home and tell Mom and Dad about the placard he received from Steve Elkington (the 1998 winner): "This thing is like one of the Ten Commandments; it is on this stone tablet, and it is pretty cool. It is definitely one of the side perks of winning here."

But Leonard knows the difference between his win at the British Open in relation to the Tournament Players Championship. "The British Open, being close to 130 years old, has the title of being a major. The TPC does not. So, there is no reason to compare apples to oranges. But this (the TPC) is one hell of an orange," said Leonard. Leonard, now 27 on the eve of the millennium, has one apple and one orange.

7:30 A.M., DECEMBER 25, 1996

Leonard did not feel phenomenal on Christmas Day in 1996. He woke up with a pain in his neck, something he was not prepared for. He quickly visited a friend who worked at Baylor's Tom Landry Center near Dallas. What he actually heard was an education about muscle science. "I remember coming away with an interest in not letting the feeling become a habit," said Leonard. A few calls later, and he became personal trainer Alison Theitje's gym rat.

Based in Kansas City, Missouri, Theitje (pronounced Tee-gee) had as his first PGA Tour client, Tom Watson. Watson credits Theitje for rejuvenating his struggling game. She was a factor in Watson winning the 1996 Memorial and finishing 25th on the Tour money list the same year.

Leonard took heed and actually started his relationship with Theitje in 1997, but did not get serious about working out until 1998. "Our goal early with Justin was to increase his strength by 100 percent," said Theitje. Take, for instance, what she claims has helped Leonard's game. "With Justin, his greatest improvement is his butt. It's an important muscle to the swing, and it's the only muscle that fires at maximum capacity."

This is great news for the 25-year-old *Cosmopolitan* magazine selection (1996) as one of the most eligible bachelors. Justin explains the selection in quantifiable terms. "They had a couple athletes in there, and I guess they were looking for somebody from golf. I guess they were going down the list and everybody on Tour is basically married. And I guess they got to the Ls and there I was, single. I mean, that's the only explanation I have," said Leonard.

For Leonard, working out has become not just a pastime. Theitje has made him an animal at the 19th hole, the gym. Leonard's cell phone rings almost daily to urge him to perform a diabolical workout. For example, Theitje tells him to go to the tennis courts at Royal Oaks for a cardio session with the pro. The tennis pro fires random shots over the net and Leonard turns into a cardio canine with a weapon (actually a tennis racket). He fetches the wayward tennis balls and hits them back to the point of beginning like a rookie. The tennis pro likes the training mode so much he just laughs a sinister laugh, standing stationary and taking it all in. Just another Theitje workout. "Oh, I've got tons of workouts like that," said Theitje.

Leonard is now hooked on protein milkshakes and has improved his overall strength close to 300 percent in some areas. His newfound attitude toward fitness reduces his stress and improves his balance. Now, the only aches and pains he feels are from exercise. "I have actually maintained my weight, I just moved the weight to the right places," said Leonard.

Smith sees the fitness from a different angle. "I honestly think it gives Justin confidence; it makes him feel better about himself." Leonard's average driving distance has increased on Tour, and it has not sacrificed his accuracy. "It really helps my balance too," he added. He is currently ranked in the top five in driving accuracy with a success rate of 78.3 percent. He credits a stronger upper body with a more stable lower body for the statistic.

At the TPC, Leonard was uncharacteristically long off the stadium course tee boxes. Whether his inspiration was increased muscle fiber or playing with John Daly in the second round is open for debate. Theitje worked her gym rat overtime after Monday and Tuesday and Leonard responded on the course. "I hit my drive on eighteen 279 yards, that's long for me," said Leonard.

As for flexibility, Leonard takes on a different approach. He joked, "I married off my sister so I could get my Stretch-mate machine in the house." In November 1997, Kelly Leonard moved out of the Dallas duplex she shared with her brother. But before she could move all her things out, she noticed what moved in. "You should see this thing, it's like a giant spiderweb. It's big. I can't even get all my things out, and he's turned my bedroom into a small gym," said Kelly Leonard.

No one has actually witnessed Leonard climb on the apparatus. A lot like the evasive superhero character Spiderman. He claims he spins poses on the bungee-materialed Stretch-mate every day when he is in town. "Oh, I get on it every time I'm in Dallas. Its wonderful for stretching and my flexibility," said Leonard. Theitje likes the advantages of the machine. "Justin wouldn't be on Tour if he didn't have great flexibility, but to keep that part of his fitness where it needs to be is also very important," she said.

Leonard's habit of working out is coupled with his habit of watching one particular Tour statistic. "As the year unfolds, I particularly watch where I stand in terms of scoring average," he said. "In my eyes, it's the most important statistic."

And his habit of working with the same teacher from his junior days until now has proved successful. Leonard's relationship with Smith has also been a catalyst for his success on Tour, but the Hogan-hatted boy wonder admits there are times when they don't meet pin-high on topics. "I think I have outgrown some things with Randy," Leonard said. "He still likes to stick his hand out there (for chipping) and won't move it until I fly a ball directly into his hand. I tell him it's about knocking the ball in the hole, not someone's hand."

Leonard respects Smith's mode of teaching. "He can do some incredible things for me," Leonard said. "But more important, he's such a good friend. He's not so concerned with my golf swing as he is about the way I'm playing, the way I'm scoring. And what's going on off the golf course."

Smith is quick to point out that Leonard had to create an unconventional grip so he could compete as a junior. Mastercard currently runs a print advertisement that shows the awkward Leonard stranglehold on the club as an eight-year-old. The grip, even back then, was not proper or priceless. In February of 1998, just before his win at the TPC, Leonard was analyzing a video of his swing. His thoughts turned immediately to the axis of the golf swing, the grip. "Randy and I were talking about my grip and how bad it was," he said. But, I had to play that way because I was smaller and trying to hit the ball farther. I think as I grew a little bit and got stronger that he saw that happening, and I went to a more conventional grip."

It was actually Leonard's senior year at Lake Highlands High School. "I remember very clearly wanting to get ready to play college golf and going to this overlap grip," Leonard said. The teacher remembers the session from a different angle. Smith readied the junior Leonard for the day when he would have to make a grip adjustment, but he did not put any pressure on his pupil. "During our sessions, he would say his ball was getting away, a little bit left. And I told him then, there is going to come a day when your grip is going to change."

Sure enough, about a month later, Leonard was back on the practice tee at Royal Oaks and he asked, "Is the time now?" Smith remembers making the initial suggestions and wanting to make a gradual turn of the hands on the club. This is where the teacher-pupil communication takes on a new plateau, kind of like an elevated green on a Nicklaus layout. About this time Smith remembers failure: "That gradual stuff turned out to be a complete bust." Smith finally told Leonard where his hands needed to be. What needed to be done was to roll his left hand farther to the left and his right hand more on top.

Smith uses this episode to relate the value of Leonard's 15th club in his bag, his mind: "Justin has always been ready. As a junior he was so in tune to improving. Justin would get down in a bunker and the sand is wet and his club bounces through the sand. He would look down at it with one of Justin's looks and say, that doesn't work the way I approached it. How am I going to make this work?"

Leonard thinks he still has the same kind of relationship with Smith. Named the 1996 PGA Club Professional of the Year, Smith has made a habit of turning the screws on Justin's golf game a little bit in different directions to make him productive. "I knew when I started with Justin that if I taught in black-and-white, I was going to get very black and white results. Instead, I was more a suggestion person. How does that feel? O.K., does that feel good? And with Justin it is real easy to tell. His eyes light up as if it were something he liked. Smith added, "When he would go silent, he was digesting in a big way. I'd ask him, does that stay in (meaning the golf swing). He'd say, that stays in."

One small facet of Leonard's game, which Smith was not instrumental in adjusting, is his pre-swing routine. Like a municipal player gauging how the club is going to make contact with the ball, Leonard cocks his club back with a strong left arm and then casually addresses the ball before starting his swing. "It gives me a sense that I need to bring the club back inside, and it started during my junior days and is something that has just become part of my full-shot routine," said Leonard. Smith liked the rehearsal. "All I know is I am hot if he doesn't do it," said Smith. He remembers only one time that Leonard's rhythm was broken in Tournament play. Ironically, "It was at the 1997 TPC at Sawgrass, and he completely busted his pre-shot timing," said

Smith. The failed preparation was short of Leonard's closing-round 78. What a difference a year makes. Leonard adopted the swing rehearsal after playing around on a tee box at a junior event.

The grip and rehearsal were two things Leonard packed for the University of Texas to play college golf. One thing he didn't pack, according to his longtime boyhood friend, Trip Kuehne, was decent apparel. "We both grew up playing junior golf with white socks with stripes on them up to our knees. But when it came to fashion, I had to educate him on what to wear," said Kuehne. He added, "Now I laugh, because I was the guy who got Justin to wear Polo."

Although Leonard's agent Vinnie Giles won't disclose the details of Leonard's endorsement deal with Polo, Kuehne might have a hard time winning an argument about the reason Leonard now wears Polo. Jeff Monday, chief of operations for the Senior Tour and one-time AJGA Tour director remembers the mighty mite as an apparel failure. "The one thing I remember about Leonard from his junior days is the big, wide white belt. I was not able to spot that at the Players Championship this year," said Monday. Leonard also packed his white bucket hat for his initial trip to Texas. The hat and the confidence were all part of his junior ensemble in the summer of 1990.

Leonard may have found fashion before he hit the University of Texas, but, on the course, his results were so fashionable, he was the first player to be named a four-time All-Southwestern Conference player. He also earned All-America honors as a senior for Jimmy Clayton. His record 17-under-par in the 1994 event tied him for the best score (271) in NCAA Tournament history with Phil Mickelson (1992).

SOMETIME IN THE NEXT MILLENNIUM

Smith has a revolving door of junior players on the Royal Oaks range. There is currently a junior player who might someday surpass all of the millennium kids, though it's too early to tell. "There are several kids who have a knack for the game," said Smith.

Introducing the millennium generation: Ford Fischer III has a game, but few Tournaments will allow him to enter. As a six-year-old at Greenhill School, he begged to compete in the seven-to-nine age group at Dallas-area junior events. Now, as an eight-year-old, he is starting to show promise. It's not fair to call an eight-year-old's game mature, but you can tell by the teacher that Smith thinks Fischer is special. "This little guy can compete. I have been fighting like crazy to put his age group on the leader board, but no luck. I will take Ford and another six-year old (Cody Grible) I'm working with and will go to Tournaments and we will toast 'em, we will just toast 'em," added Smith.

Smith teaches his students to evaluate their own shots. Fischer strikes a ball and looks at Smith. "Well," chided Smith. Fischer offered, "Ball flight a C, swing was an F." Smith counseled, "You're being too hard on yourself."

Last year, in the Games of Texas State Championship, Smith challenged Fischer to break 40. On the first day, Fischer walked up to the ninth hole and calmly asked his dad, "What do I need to shoot on this hole to shoot 39?" His dad looked at the uphill par four and said, "You need a four."

Fischer, who uses 45-inch Big Bertha driver, split the fairway. After a 7-wood approach shot, Fischer needed to get up and down to meet his goal. Fischer stroked in the 15-foot putt and said, "I want to call Randy." This is a sentiment echoed by another junior player in the mid-1980s.

Looking for a different challenge, Fischer entered the Golf Channel long-drive competition. Fischer beat everyone in his age group (seven-and eight-year-olds) by 33 yards, and he outdistanced the older age group (nine- and ten-year olds) by 15 yards.

In the Texas-Oklahoma Championship, Smith's prediction of going to statewide Tournaments with his young players turned from fable to nonfiction. On the final day in the seven-nine-year-old division, the Tournament was reduced to two Royal Oaks Country Club range rats named Grible and Fischer. Grible had a slim, two-stroke advantage that Fischer tried to cut into on the final hole, but his approach shot came up short of the green, and he settled for second place. Fischer watched Grible accept the trophy. After the trophy presentation, the two young players walked to the car. Grible told Fischer, "I want to share this with you," showing him the trophy. Fischer, knowing that second place is sometimes hard to accept, said, "I'll win TO's next year, this is your year." As the Fischers returned home, they noticed a for sale sign at the house across the street. They found out a couple days later, their neighbor, Fred Couples, was moving to California.

Ford Fischer is just the latest example of a Randy Smith disciple starting to develop. Smith takes a pride in a one-on-one teaching arena with so many junior players. He juggles a teaching schedule with travel to some of Leonard's events. He represents the many professionals who evolved from the game at the height of the spirited Nicklaus era of the 1970s. He remembers entering his career like a military call to action. "We were the merchandisers of the game," Smith said. "We were going to merchandise our golf shops to success. We were going to sell pink shoes, pink shirts, yellow golf balls. We were going to sell, sell, sell."

The driving range is just a punch wedge from his pro shop. It's on the range where Smith does his best work. "Forget all that merchandising stuff. We got away from the most important aspect of the game. As PGA professionals, we got away from the teaching of the game. And there is a kid who brought me back to that," he said. Smith averages about 1,500 lessons a year, and about 75 percent are to junior players. Several Leonard wannabes have cropped up and tried to trim trees on the Royal Oaks range just like Justin Leonard. The latest is U.S. Junior Champion Hunter Mahan.

There is a rapport that Smith creates with his prodigies. It's a combination of spirited communication on the fundamentals of the golf swing and encouragement. Smith captivates the young players because he talks their language. "Randy captivates their interest, and he really has fun," said Leonard. When they room together at PGA Tour events, the neatnik Leonard coddles his old teacher by staying one step ahead. They have an intuitive relationship. The parade of young players at Royal Oaks has continued for more than two decades. "I told Randy several times that if you would put some cots in the cart barn, we could just have camp Royal Oaks each summer. The kids ate two or three meals there anyway," said Nancy Leonard.

Before Leonard went to the 1998 British Open to defend his claret jug, he was hitting shots off a dirt cart path near the Royal Oaks range. Out of the corner of his eye he saw Ford Fischer approaching the range. Fischer was shuffling toward the range when he veered in Leonard's direction. He couldn't figure out what Leonard was doing, so he walked up and asked, "What are you doing playing shots over here?" Leonard always likes to talk with the junior players. After having taken the same direction to where he is today, he offered not an answer, but another question to Fischer: "What do you think I'm doing?" Fischer, still with an incredulous look on his face, offered, "I guess you must be getting ready for TO's." Leonard laughed at the innocence of Fischer and remarked, "I'm getting ready for the British Open."

Fischer had heard enough, and went on his way to the range. An eight-year-old-golfer certainly knows about the oldest major around, the British Open. Fischer turned to his father and said, "I know that Tournament is not as big as TO's."

6:45 P.M., JULY 18, 1999

Justin Leonard sat in his hotel room following the four-hole playoff and pondered what might have been. The 1999 British Open started out like so many of his past triumphs. The Royal and Ancient showed little remorse in Carnoustie, Scotland, for the 1999 Open. One by one the players responded with succinct jabs at the R & A for a dastardly course setup. One by one, the same players posted astronomical numbers. Like one of Leonard's lists: complain that the fairways are too skinny, check him off. Unfair pin placement, don't bother staying around for the weekend. Smith mostly listened to Leonard Saturday night. Justin had played his way into contention, just five shots out of the lead. They laughed about the similarity to 1997. Once again he was five-shots out.

The coach's advice to his pupil was simple: "You've finished the first three acts of the four-act play; enjoy the moment on Sunday." Leonard had steadied his game the first three days (73-74-71). Never mind the scorecard, which said that par was 71. Justin Leonard's mind was set on the challenge of winning another major. He was once removed from his role as the defending champion. When asked what major he would most like to win at the start of the 1999 season, there was no hesitation, "the British Open."

As Leonard reflected on what might have happened, his thoughts turned to his second shot on the 72nd hole. Sure, the lie was good. Even though the mist had created a dampness that required him to hit a crisp shot to carry the Barry Burn. He admits he was thinking he could get his club through the ball with the precision to carry the Barry Burn. His instincts told him he needed to make birdie, which would be his last chance to move ahead of Scotsman Paul Lawrie. Having witnessed Jean Van de Velde's ball sitting safely on the 17th green, the comeback kid was at it again. This time he knew it was a calculated gamble. He hit the 3-wood, and he saw the ball disappear short and to the right of the green. Leonard's ball found the Barry Burn. "The 3-shot on 18 showed me he wasn't playing for Ryder Cup points or anything else. He was playing to win the golf Tournament," said Smith, watching as he did in 1997, locked in the bedroom of his house back in Dallas.

Leonard rebounded from his worst 3-wood of the Tournament with his greatest up-and-down. A par kept him locked in a tie with Lawrie for second place. And when Van de Velde made the most famous triple-bogey 7 on the 72nd hole of any major championship, Leonard was given new life. The one extra stroke he thought he needed would have had him cradling the claret jug just like the young boy in 1986 who fell asleep on the ride home from Oklahoma.

Leonard was a walking American flag on foreign soil. This was vintage golf, just like the make-believe golf he had played on the beaches during family vacations. Back then he would create the world's toughest par-five. Now, he was living his childhood dreams playing the toughest holes of any championship in 1999.

After three holes of the four-hole playoff, all three players were still alive. Van de Velde and Leonard were one stroke behind Lawrie, who managed to birdie 17. However, the game of inches was beginning to haunt Leonard. His birdie putt on 17 was one rotation from finding the bottom of the cup. "That was one huge rotation from changing the whole complexion of the

18," said Smith. In 1997, it was a putt of the same length that found the bottom of the cup and catapulted Leonard to victory.

Leonard had to forge ahead. He and Lawrie hit perfect tee shots on 18. Van de Velde pulled his tee shot, drew a bad lie in the left-hand rough, and had to lay up in front of the Barry Burn. Leonard knew what his approach shot meant. A birdie might win the championship, and depending on what Lawrie did, a par might get him another hole. As his second shot fell into the Barry Burn, he reflected, "I felt like I lost the Tournament twice." Two shots in the span of an hour into the Barry Burn dashed the hopes of Leonard and his U.S. fans.

Leonard, the comeback kid, the guy who lacked some of the distance but made up for it with grit, again missed being the people's choice at Carnoustie. He felt like he was back at the Phoenix Open in 1996, when Mickelson edged him in a playoff, only this was a major. When David Cone pitched a perfect game at Yankee Stadium, American fans were stoic compared to the fans in Scotland, who decided they would celebrate with a wave as the players teed off on the final playoff hole.

Second place at a major is pretty lonely. Mickelson (Pinehurst) had experienced the "payne." Duval won the Tour Championship and The Players Championship, two oranges, but not the *apple* of a major. The experience of dancing so close to another major title lit Leonard's fuse for the next millennium. Leonard had earned valuable Ryder Cup points at Carnoustie. His British Open points, coupled with his play at the Canon Greater Hartford Open (finishing tied for third), were a relief to Ben Crenshaw. "I couldn't imagine not going to Brookline without Justin," said Crenshaw.

Dallas, Texas (Summer of 1981)

Nancy Leonard remembers the local city Tournaments in Dallas. "Moms would meet, we'd have our coffee cups and here we go, around Dallas to various Tournaments," said Nancy Leonard. One summer morning she remembers having to get up before dawn for a Tournament at Tennison Park when Justin was just nine years old. The little boys would be the first to tee off, and an early tee time was the penalty. Justin remembers informing his mom that the Tennison Park driving range would not be open early enough for him to be able to get in a proper practice session. Even as a nine year old, Justin needed a good warm-up before he competed, so, Nancy Leonard and her friend Marcy Craig, packed up their sons Mark and Justin, along with their clubs, shag balls and a cup of coffee.

Once they got close to the park, they found an open field used for picnicking. The problem was that at 6:15 a.m. on a Tuesday morning, the juniors turned it into a makeshift driving range. Justin instructed his mom to stand with Mrs. Craig at the far end of the field. "Justin would motion us back farther and farther until we couldn't even see the kids, it was so dark," said the motherly fore-caddie. With the headlights of the car positioned behind the players, Nancy Leonard and Marcy Craig ventured to the end of the field with the ball bags in one hand and a cold cup of coffee in the other. Nancy Leonard looked at Craig and said, "Do you think Jack Nicklaus's mother started out this way?"

Leonard has exceeded a lot of expectations from his playing days as a nine year old at Tennison Park to his current game on the PGA Tour. Trip Kuehne remembers the evolution of Justin's game. "He was always playing catch-up as a junior. We all hit the ball a long way; Stewart Cink, Duval, Brian Bateman and myself. Justin could never hit the ball out there with us, but he was such a gritty competitor. He didn't care if he was five strokes down with five holes to play. He would look each one of us in the eye and say, 'I'm going beat you'," said Kuehne.

Leonard's gift to compete and his mind might be his best assets. He is really a throwback golfer in the next millennium. He's a golfer who was never really an awesome athlete, so he made himself more athletic. His pride is refinement in a game of millimeters. If he was a baseball player he'd be a guy who runs out every ground ball. In basketball, he would be a great free throw shooter schooled in the fundamentals. In any sport he would hustle on defense and be tactically sound to the point that he would be like a coach on the field.

In terms of preparation, no player on the PGA Tour knows preparation like Leonard preparation. Even in junior golf, his yardage books were the rage. "His yardage books were the envy of every kid in junior golf. They were like novels, works of art. I've never seen courses marked quite that way," said Bateman.

Bateman remembers in junior golf that when it came to playing a practice round, he and Trip Kuehne couldn't really count on Leonard. "Trip and I would sleep in, hang out at the hotel and we would get to the course by 10:30 a.m. Justin would be finishing up his round. At the Junior Classic, we were hitting balls, and here was Justin walking up the 18th, writing something down in that damn yardage book," said Bateman.

Smith likens his approach to Tour life in the same way. He never misses an opportunity to stay systematic. But, Smith insisted, "He's not point A to point B. He enjoys cutting up." But, as far as his habits, "You know on Sunday he's going to come in and get all of his stuff put away at the hotel. Tuesday at a specific time he's going to be at the golf course, have breakfast, situate his locker, and he will play the golf course. He never misses a practice tee on Tuesday afternoon. Pro-am on Wednesday, his success is rooted in organization," said Smith. Apple order for the apple-pie "kid" on Tour. From the tempo of his golf swing to his organization, Leonard's timing is a big part of his game plan.

The essence of Leonard is the intangible; however, even in junior golf, the statistics did not warrant a bright future. "If you check out my record, I never won a lot of Tournaments. The thing about junior golf for me is that I learned that I enjoyed the competition, and I learned the rules of the game," said Leonard. He observed the Mickelsonian way, he played junior and college golf with David Duval and he filed every gigabyte of information away. Randy Smith swears his brain is like a little computer. "Some stuff sticks and some stuff, he just discards," said Smith. But when the competition heats up, especially in July and August, Leonard's vision is 3-D. Check out his scores at Carnoustie, Winged Foot and Royal Troon. It may be one early-season Tournament in 1996, the Phoenix Open, that showed Leonard's true competitive spirit.

In a playoff with Phil Mickelson, Leonard "was like a dog on Mickelson's leg, he couldn't shake him off," said Smith. Mickelson eventually won the playoff, but Leonard played through the (Mickelsonian) partisan Phoenix gallery noise and the course to show his competitiveness. "Looking back, I think I learned a lot about myself and learned probably as much as I would have learned by winning it," said Leonard.

Mark Fidrych was a great young pitcher for the Detroit Tigers in the late 1970s and early 1980s. His ability to talk to the ball branded him an oddity as a professional athlete. Justin Leonard did not stand on the first playoff hole at Carnoustie and talk to his Titleist. But, as the game is waged between the ears like no other, Leonard has reverted to an age-old prescription— self-talking. Like so many golfers, he talks to his golf ball in the air, but he talks to himself even more. His self-communication is one reason he handles the pressure of major competition. "He doesn't beat himself up, but he gets his mind focused a lot of times," said Smith. And while his caddie Riefke is his soul mate on the fairways, Leonard also commands his mind to certain on-course objectives: "I do talk to myself on the golf course. Actually I've got a friend, Fran Piersola, that I talk to occasionally. My mental approach is an important part of the game for me. Fran gives me an idea of ways to generate successful self-talk. It is more for reassurance that the self-talking I'm doing is the right thing."

Now the other PGA Tour players are talking about the kid from Dallas with the game. His fitness regimen has them whispering about his increased length off the tee. His average driving distance has crept up the statistical charts. Since he came on the PGA Tour, he has been labeled a shorter hitter. He has carried the reputation like a scoring stanchion down the fairway.

He's come a long way since his missed tee time in Denver in 1987, but the Meridian golf links, with its British links-style design was a cyclical beginning. First came the 1992 U.S. Amateur title, then the 1994 NCAA title. Leonard has one of the best records in the majors over the past three years, as well as a spot on the 1997 and 1999 Ryder Cup teams. He is starting to put check marks next to the items on his lists.

He recently did a public service advertisement for the PGA Tour called the "silent fan." The piece features Leonard curling in a 30-foot putt on the 18th hole. Because of the special effects, the film crew did not need for Leonard to actually make the long-distance putt. They were able to have him hit about a three-footer so they could track the ball along the same line from where he would begin the putt. In a polite, gentlemanly way, he said, "Guys, I am going to make the putt from here." He has a competitiveness and big aspirations.

Big is also the reason Leonard earned two middle names. "My parents were between giving me the middle names of Charles or Garrett, my grandparents, two different people," said Leonard. "I was eight lbs., 12 ounces, so they said, he's a big kid, might as well give him two names." He also responds to Just, Justin, Jasper and anything that starts with a "J." He has arrived on the PGA Tour just in time to send the game into the next millennium.

GROOVY DUUVY

Like most years on the PGA Tour, the pastoral playground known as Augusta National marks the true beginning of the year. In 1989, there was something in the rarefied Augusta air that heightened the usual suspense surrounding the Masters Tournament, and it involved a golfer named Scott Hoch.

It's never easy being green or trying to wear green. The predecessor to the king-like reputation for second-place finishes, Hoch spent a Sunday in April examining a short putt, which would be his ticket to greendom and the green jacket. All that stood between him and a visit to Butler Cabin was a ticklish 18-inch putt for par on the second playoff hole. Eighteen inches separated Hoch from his breakthrough. As the sun faded into the Augusta dogwoods, Hoch's gimme putt rimmed out, and his name became immortalized as the player to come *closest* to winning a major. His last name became forever linked with a key component of an engine throttle, which, in the modern golfing dictionary means succumbed to pressure. With Nick Faldo wearing green, Hoch was green with envy. Ten years later, the putt still haunts Hoch, a player who has won eight times on Tour and over $9 million, but no majors.

This same summer, on a younger playing field, the national junior circuit, typical greenside golf vernacular was quickly changing from *Caddyshack*'s "Miss it, Noonan," to Augusta's real-life yip, "Don't Scott CHOCH it." A 17-year-old had little time to throw a fishing line at the TPC Sawgrass stadium course waters because he was spending a lot of time at AJGA and USGA junior Tournaments. It was his summer to leave the Timuquana Country Club range behind and face other challenges, such as getting ready for college golf at Georgia Tech. He had just signed a letter of intent to play for coach Puggy Blackmon, and Duval was too busy to pay attention to what was unfolding at golf's major league level. He had his white bucket hat with the blue cord stripes pulled down tight. He really had his mental blinders on.

Never mind that Tom Kite was tossing away the U.S. Open at Oak Hill. Who really cared that Greg Norman would miss an opportunity at the British Open at Royal Troon? Stephen King was writing the script at the PGA Championship. Mike Reid, nicknamed "Radar" for his accuracy off the tee, pulled a Corporal Klinger. With a three-stroke lead and three holes to play, Reid pulled a drive into the lake on the 16th hole at Kemper Lakes, and that was only the start. A stubbed chip on 17, followed by a stabbed "tap-in." Reid dropped three strokes in fifteen minutes and completed the year's sweep of *major* disappointments.

The golfing world seemed like it was on a losing streak in 1989. Even a golfing manufacturer named Ping was taking a backseat as it became embroiled in a not-so-groovy square grooves controversy over its Ping Eye two-irons. While Ping was protecting its grooves, there was a groovy right-hander, nicknamed Duuvy, who was doing his best to make people forget about a certain left-hander from San Diego. In June, Phil Mickelson, the valedictorian of the junior golf ranks the previous three summers, was etching his name on the NCAA Championship Trophy. On the kid's circuit, David Duval saw a void.

The summer temperatures were just heating up when Duval descended on El Cajon, California, for the USGA Junior Championship. He made match play, six strokes off the medalist pace (151). In the second and third rounds, he beat two kids from Dallas named Trip Kuehne (3 and 2) and Justin Leonard (4 and 2). Chris Riley was a home-state favorite in the semifinals. The blond Floridian beat Riley (3 and 2). In the championship, Duval prevailed with a 1-up victory over Austin Maki.

Duval captured his first national win. A week earlier, he defeated Aaron Crewse in a playoff to win in America's heartland at Otter Creek in Indiana. Even though Otter Creek had the best players from the Midwest, the USGA Junior was the Tour Championship of Junior Golf. Two thousand and twenty-five kids entered the Junior Championship, and Duval was left holding the trophy. Duval headed straight from the USGA Junior to the AJGA Boys' Junior at the TPC at Las Colinas, in Irving, Texas, also the site of the Byron Nelson Classic. Again, he dominated the field, shooting 68-76-72-71. Three starts, three wins.

"He came in that summer (1989) and said 'game over,' I'm here," said AJGA executive director, Stephen Hamblin. Hamblin and his staff likened Duval's quiet demeanor that summer to a focused teenager with an "edge." Duval traveled to Tournaments, and in many ways he was a world once removed from his friends at Episcopal High School. They were going to proms and graduating, while he flew from Indiana to California to Texas and then, finally, home.

The junior ranks were erasing the name Phil Mickelson, and they were beginning to get used to a long-haired Florida surfer-looking dude nicknamed Duuvy. Duval's streak of 1989 was something Mickelson never accomplished. Duval was a year behind Mickleson, and although he won the Plantation Junior Classic and was named to the AJGA first team in 1988, it was Mickelson who continued to get top honors.

Georgia Tech head golf coach Puggy Blackmon remembers counseling his top recruit when he first came to Atlanta. "He was always kind of in Phil's shadow. I kept trying to tell David during the recruitment process that your learning curves will intersect." Sure enough, with the season-ending AJGA Tournament of Champions, a Tournament Mickelson owned from 1986 to 1988, Duuvy got his groove back.

His play at the Palm Beach Polo Club was extraordinary. The kid from Jacksonville didn't smile much. "Kids thought if you talked to him, he would bite your head off," remembers junior and later Nike Tour comrade Harry Rudolph. Duval shot 71-71-73 and edged future Yellow Jacket Stewart Cink by one stroke to win. In a period of less than a month (July 20 to August 14) Duval won four Tournaments. It was a remarkable streak, but it marked a refreshing changing of the guard on the junior circuit. The Mickelsonian dominance of 1988 had been evaporated, like dew from the greens, to the college game. Groovy Duuvy was staking claim as the boy of summer in 1989.

The Tournament of Champions win also meant Duval didn't have to go home for Thanksgiving. He would be named the 1989 AJGA Player of the Year at Innisbrook in Tarpon Springs, Florida.

Hamblin was accustomed to introducing the Player of the Year awards at Innisbrook. He enjoyed offering jokes as an entry into the top awards for the girls and boys. Only this year, it wasn't the talkative left-hander from San Diego accepting the honor. Duval, the free-spirited introvert, was about to receive the highest honor in the junior game. The Vardon trophy for "kids," was about to go to the bucket-hatted birdie machine with the 'tude.

An atmosphere of nearly giddy nervousness pervaded the capacity banquet hall crowd. Expectations from the juniors and parents in attendance were that Duval's Player of the Year acceptance speech might be the shortest in history, not unlike the way he hit a tee shot, grabbed his bag, and sauntered down the fairway. As it turned out, groovy Duuvy did a *carpe diem*. He cradled the award and began to settle in for a succinct jab at the organization that was honoring him and the evening's decorum. Instead of grabbing the highest award in junior golf and heading for his seat, Duval did something he rarely ever did. He smiled. His grin said it all, as he began:

"I just want everybody to know that it wasn't easy. This organization, the AJGA, did not even accept my application for the first three Tournaments I entered," said Duval.

A joke from Duval was like a duck-hook, out-of-bounds. The crowd appreciated the unexpected humor. Parents attending the formal affair roared their appreciation for the Georgia Tech freshman. They all understood exactly what Duval was saying. Sometimes the toughest part of the AJGA was getting chosen for a Tournament field. It was not that the organization chose the field haphazardly; the junior game was changing fast, and it was difficult to compare grassroots programs from every corner of America and internationally. Disgruntled parent phone calls were a reality Hamblin and his staff dealt with daily.

The summer of 1989 was one of brutal ironies in the world of golf. While Duval grooved into a streak of success on the junior boys' level, Hoch, Kite, Norman, and Reid were dealt major blows that affected each player's career.

"GROOVIN'...ON A SUNDAY AFTERNOON."
—THE RASCALS

Colonial Williamsburg has preserved the tradition of life dating back to America's early settlers. Battlegrounds, cobblestone streets, hand-carved wooden furniture, symbols speak of the way life used to be before things like titanium shafts and the Tommy Hilfiger blimp. Williamsburg is a wooden-shafted mashie, brassie and niblick kind of town, built on the remnants of old-town colony life.

When Richard Kingmill, an English colonist, founded a plot of land along the James River in 1736, he had a vision. He saw an opportunity to develop a colony, which would serve as the vibrant capital of the New World. Known as the flower of the new world, Williamsburg became the largest and the most populous colony. Then, almost 50 years after the colony had been established, Thomas Jefferson decided to move the capital of the common man to Richmond, leaving Williamsburg to a more mundane existence. It was not known at the time, but this move preserved the momentous beginning for tiny Williamsburg. It became a historical treasure.

Golf has been a part of the Williamsburg area since 1947, when the Williamsburg Inn opened a nine-hole course. Exactly half a century later, it was the stage for the Michelob Championship at Kingsmill. Some players play it because Kingsmill along the James River is Curtis Strange's backyard. Many Tour grinders see the event as an opportunity to win, because many of the top 30 money winners are at home preparing for the end-of-the-year premiere events like the Tour Championship.

In 1997, David Duval arrived in Williamsburg, much like our early pioneers. He had the tools of a great player, but he also carried a burden. For Duval, burdens on and off the course had been like dimples on his Titleist Professional 90 golf ball. This burden weighed more heavily on Duval's evaluators than on the shoulders of the 25-year-old. Verbal tattoos like the Buffalo Bill of the PGA Tour just stoked his internal flame to compete. Having played in 86 PGA Tour events, he had nary a win.

He had nearly won earlier in the season at Pebble Beach, and again at the Bell-South. At Pebble Beach he opened with a 65, came back with a 71, and then fired a third-round 62 to tie the course record. As he looks back, it was so clear. "I really thought I had to shoot a 63 or 64 in the final round to win," said Duval.

His final-round 71 left him one stroke off Mark O'Meara's winning margin. He was left to share second place with Tiger Woods. Woods was just warming up for his record-setting run at Augusta in April. And O'Meara was supposed to win at Pebble Beach. He had made a habit of winning at Pebble Beach (1989, 1990 and 1992). It was partly because of his success at Pebble Beach that Jamie Diaz of *Sports Illustrated* labeled O'Meara with the distinction as the "King of the B's," meaning the master of the unimportant Tournaments. That would obviously change in 1998 with his dueling majors at the Masters and the British Open.

And at the Bell-South, Duval was tied with Scott McCarron after 66 holes of the event, but then he watched as McCarron made birdies on 13 and 15. The former Yellow Jacket was stung by a bogey on 16, which gave McCarron a three-shot margin of victory. Duval did not collect the runner-up stamp of notoriety by just missing at the Bell-South and Pebble Beach, though. Duval "almost" won the Bell South as an amateur at the age of 20. It was again his final round, a 79, that was his undoing. Even in his rookie PGA Tour season, his "almost won" list included the Memorial, Pebble Beach and the Bob Hope Chrysler Classic (he would get revenge here in 1999). Eleven times he finished either second or third coming into Williamsburg.

It was Puggy Blackmon who pondered his young challenger's dilemma. "Why hasn't David Duval won?" To Blackmon, the answer was simple: few people knew the guts of Duval. Few knew his inner drive and perseverance like Blackmon. "He's always just been like a fox in a hen house, or even better, a light switch in a dark room. Once you find it and know where it is, there are not many PGA Tour players who are going to get much sleep," said Blackmon.

Duval showed up in Williamsburg trying to forge his way out of a trench-like reputation for being a talented 20-something player and, wait—the gallery is silent—shhh, "a second-place finisher." A guy who battled all week only to win a big paycheck, without saying checkmate. Similar to so many pioneers and explorers who thought that might happen if they went beyond the physical realm of geography. Duval was not worried about dropping off the map in Williamsburg. He was more worried about righting his playing ship, which was not on a Mayflower-type navigational course.

In September, he missed cuts at the LaCantera Open (72-74) and the B.C. Open (70-75). "I don't think I ever missed three cuts in a row on the Tour, and now I was going to the Buick Challenge where I had never made a cut, so something had to give," said Duval. He stabilized his ship with a top-ten finish at the Buick Challenge when he shot a 6-under-par 66 in the final round. Even though Duval finished tied for ninth he says, "It might be the best I hit the ball all year. I was really on that week."

Duval then arrived near the battlegrounds in Eastern Virginia and he was ready to do battle. He was in a feisty mood, when he usually plays his best golf. "In college, the worse his mood, the better he played," said Blackmon.

Duval's opening-round 67 at Kingsmill was typical. Early-round Duval par busters at Pebble Beach (65), Phoenix (66), the Houston Open (65), the Bell South (66), the Colonial (66) were commonplace that year. Based on his early-season Tournament showing, Duval knew a low early round meant little when it came to grabbing the Sunday crystal. With Duval's temperament set at even keel with a pinch of anger, he was on the verge of becoming the unexpected Sunday hero. It was the evolution of Duval's game, coupled with a brewing temperament that was danger for the rest of the PGA Tour.

Duval's eagle on the par-5 15th meant he had a three-stroke lead with three to play. This margin, three strokes, was the same lead Duffy Waldorf enjoyed to start the day, so Duval kept plotting his resilient course. Grant Waite was also making a charge. The New Zealander, tied with Duval in second to start the day, made four consecutive birdies and finished with a 67. Waldorf rode a final round like he was down the road at Busch Gardens on a roller coaster. After making birdies on 14, 15, and 16, he sweated his way into a playoff with a good up-and-down par on 18. Three players (Duval, Waldorf, and Waite) were now tied at 13-under 271.

That is when it happened. The normally presidential Virginia crowd began to combust in support of the kid. It was as if Williamsburg native Bruce Hornsby was playing the piano on the 18th tower and they were about to rock the rock star-looking twenty-something player. He may not have heard the boats in the James off the 17th green, but they were blowing their horns for the guy without a PGA Tour win.

The three players stood on the 18th tee, and Duval seized the moment with a symphonic drive over 300 yards. His tee shot left him with just a 9-iron to the green. Waite's approach shot came up short of the green and Waldorf was left scrambling from a poor tee shot. Duval finally felt the inertia of the crowd. "It just seemed like they were behind me. It seemed like they were just pulling for me." Pulling for the guy with the Darth Vader-like Oakley sunglasses and the goatee? Virginians pulling for a kid from ACC foe Georgia Tech? Duval was hateable. Fans couldn't see the whites of his eyes. He had the scowl and the sneer down like a bad habit.

When his 10-foot birdie putt dropped in the hole, so did some emotions and burdens. Birdies and burdens were all that Duval ever knew. As he looked around to accept the moment, his look was one of accomplishment. Not fulfillment, but accomplishment. Duval had won his first PGA Tour event. It was not a major, but it was a major hurdle. He had broken through. He still references the win. Even after he shot 59 in the final round of the 1999 Bob Hope Chrysler Classic, he would say, "The day I won in Williamsburg was still one of the greatest days of golf I have ever had. I really embrace that day."

The heart of a champion? A 27-year-old almost shoots his age on the back nine and he wants to preserve his historic first win at a small colonial town in Virginia? Part of Duval's breakthrough had to be credited with the newest member of team Duval, his caddy Mitch Knox. At the bequest of his old Georgia Tech teammate, Charlie Rymer, Duval had hired Knox in August. Jeff Weber, Duval's caddy and friend dating back to his Nike days, was let go. The new team-on-the-verge had passed a barrier.

David Duval had broken through before Williamsburg. Before, it was a breakaway from a childhood filled with strife and anger and college days that were sometimes filled with resentment and isolation. When he realized on the Nike Tour that golf was going to be a business, he gained confidence. For groovy Duuvy, this was a beginning, the genesis of the way it was supposed to be.

A self-proclaimed "introvert" who makes the term "guarded" seem like a coming-out party, Duval's emotions were kept in check. He enjoyed his first win privately. "I felt my time would come. Other people wanted to make a bigger deal out of not winning right away," said Duval. The burden to win was somebody else's burden.

Perseverance was a well-kindled Duval moniker. "I've never gotten off to quick starts in junior golf, college golf, or amateur golf," he said. Duval was not ready to bask in the glow of Monday headlines. His light was on, but he was a player bent on continuing to work on his game. It wasn't just his game that was beginning to turn, it was his life.

Ralph Waldo Emerson once said, "Men achieve a certain greatness unawares, when working to another aim." Duval was playing golf, but that was just part of his journey. He was also building bridges spiritually with his family, and with a close relationship, girlfriend Julie MacArthur. Blackmon presided over it all, and at times kept it from crashing in on David Duval the person, not David Duval the PGA Tour phenom. "David walks to his own drummer. He is a loner who never trusted a lot of people. It took a while with me," said Blackmon.

His mentor from his days at Georgia Tech had watched Duval grow up, away from the golf course. "We worked on a lot with David; it started with never changing his demeanor; but he needed to respect people a little bit more away from the course."

It did not take Duval long to build on his first win. The Michelob Championship at Kingsmill wasn't the Super Bowl, but Duval may as well have made the usual post-big-game-victory endorsement, "I'm going to Disney World." His first win propelled him to "Tomorrowland" and the PGA Tour's next stop, the Walt Disney World Golf Classic.

On Sunday, it was beginning to look like a small world after all. After 72 holes, Duval and Dan Forsman were tied at 270, one stroke better than his effort in Virginia. Back to 18 for another playoff. Both players hit their approach shots wayward on the first playoff hole, Duval into a bunker left of the green and Forsman short on the collar. Forsman chunked his chip shot, which barely made it to the green. Then, he missed a 25-foot par putt. After an average bunker play, Duval rolled in a 15-foot par putt for his second straight victory.

The post-Tournament festival featured Duval kissing Minnie Mouse and hugging Mickey. Not since Billy Andrade won two times in 1991 had a player recorded back-to-back wins on the PGA Tour. He called the second win part of finding his "comfort level." Whether it was Zen visualization, a comfort level, or just plain good golf didn't really matter. What Duval proved is that he could close the deal. Most of the players in the year-end Tour Championship were at home during Disney, monitoring the progress of the golden boy with the game.

Three wins in a row just doesn't happen on the PGA Tour unless you head back to the seventies and another blond bomber named Jack Nicklaus. The game had always been trademarked by the top names, and more than anything, Duval wanted an identity. What better way to get an identity than with a Nicklaus-type streak? Duval showed up on the PGA Tour in 1995 looking a lot like Nicklaus did in 1962. Pudgy, with a gleam in his eyes and powering the golf ball.

"I AM A SLOW WALKER, BUT I NEVER WALK BACK." —ABRAHAM LINCOLN

With two wins in 1997, Duval did not want to walk back to his image as a Tour up-and-comer. His attitude was not charismatic, but businesslike. At the Tour Championship, the best 30 businessmen in the industry would tee it up. Duval knew he would have to turn his game up a notch at the Champions Golf Club in Houston. At the Tour Championship, he somehow managed to place his two prior wins aside and accept the challenge. He made it three in a row by beating one of the best fields of the year. Davis Love said, "He's been there. David has been close a lot of times. A lot of people talked about how he couldn't finish. He's proven over the last month that he can. I think he will be doing it for a long time."

Love knew something about streaks. In 1992, he won three PGA Tour events in a month when he won the Tournament Players Championship, the MCI Heritage and the K-mart Greater Greensboro Open. Through Duval's end-of-the-season navigation, he made $1,269,000. His last nine PGA Tour paychecks of 1997 told the story. He went from making $8,497 by finishing tied for 48th at the U.S. Open to a trifecta ($279,000; Williamsburg), ($270,000; Disney World), to ($720,000; the Tour Championship). After going 86 Tournaments without a win, the kid from Jacksonville was 3-0. "I am not going to give the money back, but the real satisfaction comes from beating a field like this," said Duval. The right words at the right time for the right-hander from Jacksonville. Duval, mature well beyond his years on the course, knew something about streaks. In 1989 he had a winning streak in junior golf. Now eight years later, he was groovin' on Sunday afternoons.

In its 1998 January issue, *Golf Digest* proclaimed that 1997 was the year of the Tiger. Not obsessed with the spotlight, Duval fed off the headlines. It was the little things that were stoking his cerebral furnace. He knew that Tiger's emotions were wider than the tee markers on the PGA Tour. He also knew the value of a Zen-like existence. He was content playing out his streak and keeping his focus. Duval understood the power of a mental perspective. He had built his life one brick at a time, not letting outside influences trigger emotional responses. That was Tiger's game. Duval, shaped by Blackmon and Rotella, was a volcano of emotions on the inside.

In sports, there are winning streaks, losing streaks, and just plain streaks. Duval's life has been a combination of both. "David always thought he had to do it all himself. He grew up in a difficult situation. Why or how could anybody else help him?" said Puggy Blackmon. The PGA Tour player in the glass bubble sometimes played lonely. Blackmon said, "The attitude of David Duval is, when it's time to put the tee in the ground, nobody else is out there playing. Nobody is on the golf course." Focused? Forget it. Duval never trusted anyone growing up, and his attitude on the course reflects his independence

There is nature, nurture, and then there is the Duval upbringing. As a nine-year-old, Duval was just a hanger-on at Timuquana Country Club in Jacksonville. His dad, the head pro, would send his son to the range to beat range balls with his older brother, Brent.

In what seemed like the amount of time it took to hit a bucket of balls, his brother became sick. They all thought Brent just needed some quick energy—a few iron pills, rest, and he'd be O.K. What they discovered was that Brent had a disease called aplastic anemia. For the Duvals, the disease was a quick learning process. Aplastic anemia went from medical journal dictionary to the dinner table. The doctors were succinct in their diagnosis: the best chance at treating the disease was through a bone marrow transplant.

The doctors quickly identified David as the most innocent, but potentially the most successful, donor. Transferring bone marrow from David, a high-percentage match, was the life ring that gave Brent hope. This was like a match-play event David did not understand at the time. How could he be expected to grasp the gravity of his big brother's illness? A nine-year-old was supposed to be playing Little League and entering junior golf Tournaments, not lying down on a sterile hospital bed, having doctors tell him it wasn't going to hurt.

Brent went through chemotherapy to prepare for the bone marrow transfer. David watched helplessly as his brother, who just a short time ago was hitting balls on the range with him, was plugged into machines, pale and lifeless. Brent soon lost his fight with the disease. His brother's bone marrow did not stop the chaos inside his body.

What had happened inside Brent seemed to pervade the Duval home. David's parents, Diane and Bob, divorced about a year after Brent died. David was left searching for answers, but he was caught in the middle of bitterness resulting from a family's painful struggle to come to grips with the loss of a child. It had pulled apart so much. David had a muddled ambivalence toward the way life was supposed to be. One way he coped with the pain was to keep beating range balls into the humid Jacksonville breeze at Timuquana. After his dad left, his mother turned to alcohol to ease the pain. David's game was beginning to develop, but his home was a mosaic of self-pity, anger, and despair.

Was this going to be a losing streak in life? Duval learned at an early age that winning streaks, and more important losing streaks, eventually end. He grew up communicating with his dad through golf instead of words. "I think in some ways he wanted to be better than his dad. He had a pretty high mark to shoot for in terms of golf," said Blackmon. "Because of what happened to his brother, David grew up a private person. Most of his friends were his dad's friends."

Bob Duval was a classic teacher of the game, who had enough game to play competitively, but instead created a country club vocation—captain's choice events, club championships, merchandising the pro shop was the routine. Bob Duval was a country club pro for 28 years before he got his chance to compete on the PGA Senior Tour. He wanted to test his game against the best, and he tried to qualify for several U.S. Opens. He missed three years in a row by just three strokes each time. His thinking was, "If I can't beat David, why would I want to play in the Open?" His son was his measuring stick. As his son's teacher, the father wanted David to take advantage of opportunities he bypassed.

What does David think about his dad's travails? David said, "I don't think you can give him enough credit."

"EDUCATION IS NOT THE FILLING OF THE PAIL, BUT THE LIGHTING OF A FIRE."
—WILLIAM BUTLER YEATS

Freshman orientation wasn't easy for Duval. Instead of finding the library, he wanted to know what University of Texas great Ben Crenshaw once echoed to longtime University of Texas golf coach George Hannon, "Where's the first tee, and what's the course record?" The unapologetic Duval wanted to know what it was going to take to play number one. Senior Charlie Rymer was coming off an incredible junior season, where he led the team to the Southern Intercollegiate Championship and garnered medalist honors. He was an honorable-mention All-American and the cog in the Ramblin' Wreck golf machine. "With David coming in, I thought it would fire Charlie up. Charlie just went belly up and David dominated," said Puggy Blackmon.

Duval didn't win an event his freshman year; in fact, he didn't win anything until the spring of his sophomore year. He missed winning the ACC Tournament his freshman year by one stroke. He didn't have to look far for comfort, finishing second in the ACC Tournament. Curtis Strange (1976), Lanny Wadkins (1970, 1971), Gary Hallberg (1979) and Davis Love III (1983) all were second-place finishers in the conference Tournament. A second-place finish as a freshman may have been an omen for his game on the PGA Tour, but he was more concerned with bigger things. Finishing second wasn't good enough for Duval. While Duval began to burn like a hot ember in college golf, Rymer flickered out. "Charlie fell madly in love with the girl he eventually married, and his mind was not in it," said Blackmon.

Duval finished off his freshman year with a top 10 in the East Regional and the NCAA Championship, which took place at Innisbrook—the site of his rousing acceptance speech. From Thanksgiving until early summer, Duval had come full circle. From the king of the Kids to a freshman with a good game, he maintained the same attitude. He was named an All-American, an honor he would repeat three more times (only Mickelson and Gary Hallberg were named All-American four years). He also successfully alienated a Georgia Tech team, which apparently had at one time a crucial team component—chemistry.

In Blackmon's system, the players earned their stripes. "Even as a three-time All-American, David had to come in and earn his spot," said Blackmon. The college coach who helped get the national junior scene started in 1978 with Mike Bentley was firm on making statements. He was a practice player's dream and a Tournament player's nightmare. If you played at Georgia Tech during the Blackmon tenure, you knew you were only as good as the last qualifier.

Duval as a young college player liked the prime time, but rules were rules. The player who qualified sixth wasn't supposed to go to Tokyo and compete in the Shiseido Cup. Tournament organizers changed the rules. Not only did the U.S. Junior Champion make the trip, there was suddenly a great wall dividing the team in the Far East. Duval's scores would not count toward the team at the event. This would not have been a big deal if he had just finished in the middle of the pack, but Duval did not know middle of the pack. He was getting a chance to compete face-to-face with Phil Mickelson the *dandy left-handy from Sandyago*. Mickelson's sliding 30-footer on the 18th hole was all that separated Duval from the individual title. In a little less than six months, Georgia Tech went from the NCAA golf team with the best chemistry to being driven by a mad chemist. Duval was acid to a team that was hitting the brink.

With Blackmon's team coming undone, he diverted the team's interest—which started with Rymer and Duval—to the gym. He decided fitness was going to be a part of the program. At the behest of the coach, both Duval and Rymer checked into the athletic trainer's office for a body-fat test. "I wanted to get both of them down a lot. We put Charlie in and it was like the Pillsbury Dough boy. David wasn't that bad." Yet. Blackmon met up with Duval during the Nike Tour swing in 1993 and remembered kidding Duval that he was meeting Rymer too often at the Golden Corral buffet. "David always told me, coach, I am wearing the same size pants that I did in college." Blackmon never answered, but he thought to himself, "Yeah, but they are a lot tighter."

Blackmon never played games with Duval; instead, he met the person head-on. The relationship developed partly because Duval wasn't going to get along with any of his other Georgia Tech teammates. "We had some pretty good run-ins," Blackmon remembered. "I wanted to be close to David, yet there was a coach-player relationship that had boundaries. I sometimes don't think David understood those boundaries." Soon, there were two golf teams at Georgia Tech—Blackmon and Duval, and the rest of the Yellow Jacket golfers, Mike Clark, Tripp Isenhour, and Rymer.

Defending Duval was part of Blackmon and Bob Rotella's challenge. They designed old-fashioned encounter sessions with the entire team. "I felt there was a lot of animosity. Because when you have a group of egos involved in a golf team, there is jealousy," said Blackmon. Blackmon counseled Duval on the fact that he "wasn't going to win a national championship alone." Blackmon saw the influence his player had on the rest of the team, but it wasn't as readily apparent to Duval. Blackmon said Rotella sat Duval down and said, "David, you can choose to make comments to really inflate the confidence of your teammates or you can really deflate them. Your opinion carries a lot of weight, and they are affected by everything you do."

Blackmon looks back on the sessions with his team as a learning process. "Bob (Rotella) told me that I could sit back and not deal with it. David was like a thoroughbred," said Blackmon. Duval looks back on the Georgia Tech days as a growing-up period.

One of the nation's most respected golf coaches, Jim Brown at Ohio State, remembers witnessing Duval's freshman campaign with admiration: "He reminded me of John Cook because he played above his years. When Cook came in as a freshman, he played like a senior. The same with David. He had been through all the wars already, nothing was going to bother him. He had the game, the desire and the determination to be one of the best."

As Duval's consistency evolved on the course, the team slowly unraveled even farther. The boiling point came at the NCAA East Regionals at the Yale Golf Course in 1991, Duval's sophomore year. Blackmon remembered: "My best player wants to figuratively beat up his own teammates in the parking lot. College golf was supposed to be a team sport. And my guys didn't want to eat at the same restaurant, they wanted no part of my best player."

Rotella's answers were always simple compared to the complexity of the problems. Blackmon remembers hearing Rotella credos, which included, "golf being a game of composure. And free will is a golfer's greatest strength and power." Blackmon had seen Duval part the waters as a freshman, and it was now getting worse. At the regionals, Duval tried to warm up to his teammates. He joined the rest of the team for breakfast. He was uncharacteristically nice and pleasant. Blackmon thought, "Wow, this is a change." Duval went out and shot 73, not a great round from the premier prima donna in the college game. Rotella urged

Blackmon to let David be David. Duval lathered up an attitude for the second round. He shot 65 and double-bogeyed the 9th hole. "Thank God for Bob Rotella," said Blackmon. "He helped both David and me get through the college years."

"COWARDICE, AS DISTINGUISHED FROM PANIC, IS ALMOST ALWAYS SIMPLY A LACK OF ABILITY TO SUSPEND THE FUNCTIONING OF THE IMAGINATION." —ERNEST HEMINGWAY

Duval was awarded the opportunity to play in his first major in 1990. By winning the previous summer's USGA Boys' Junior, Duval, then 19, was going to tee it up with the PGA Tour elite at Medinah Country Club's No. 3 course, in Chicago. When Blackmon arrived to caddy for his freshman, Duval was asleep at the hotel. Duval woke up with one thing on his mind; his caddie for the week was going to carry a big professional-style bag. If he was going to play at the major-league level, he needed to look like a major leaguer, not a glorified junior player.

The player and volunteer coach/caddie had another Rotella-like encounter session, only this one was over the size of the golf bag. Blackmon was a college golf coach, not a professional caddie and definitely not a pack mule. David did not waste time letting coach know his preference: "I want you to carry the big bag." Blackmon responded by succinctly telling Duval, "I'm carrying the small bag because that's what you paid for."

Duval was paired with Brad Faxon the first two days. Blackmon remembered Faxon from his playing days at Furman. He had also worked with Rotella. Faxon showed his game by shanking his drives on the first two holes. Blackmon remembers the lesson he tried to impart: "I remember telling David, check out Faxon, he hit it all over the ranch the first two days and shot even par, this is the stuff Rotella is talking about. Here is a case study in perseverance. Does that show you something?" Duval hit his groove early. He birdied three of the first six holes he played and eventually made the 36-hole cut. Faxon remembers this about the blonde collegian: "He played a little slow and wasn't too sure of what he was doing. He was definitely green. But, he powered the golf ball. And he never showed any emotion." Duval wasn't intimidated by the words "major" or "U.S. Open." From that Tournament on, David and Blackmon created a relationship based on trust. They shared Duval's player's badge so they could both eat the Medinah breakfast buffet. "That week was where we established a great relationship," reflected Blackmon. "I am just another resource for him."

Medinah did a lot of things for Duval in 1990. It gave him an early measuring stick of where he was as a player against the world's best. "I think David, like most players, questioned where he was in terms of becoming a great player," said Blackmon. Success on a U.S. Open course against the best professionals in the world was a pretty good start. Hale Irwin beat Mike Donald in a playoff to win at Medinah, but Duval had played well enough to make the cut, and that alone was a cornerstone accomplishment.

In the final round, Duval was paired with David Frost. It was evident to both Duval and Blackmon that Frost wanted to get the round over and get out of Chicago. Duval was caught playing faster than normal—a "David Frost pace." His game subsequently came undone on the back nine. Blackmon finally said, "Either you're going to slow down your pace, or I'm going to walk slower and you're going to have to wait on me at the ball."

After both Frost and Duval hit in a greenside bunker on 17, Blackmon was raking the trap so that it was carefully prepared for the next group. When he finished, grabbed the small bag, and got to the next tee, his prodigy was seething over his play. Noticing a speck of dirt on one of his irons, Duval pulled the damp white towel from around Blackmon's neck. Snapping his head forward, the embarrassed caddie couldn't believe the action and contemplated the best approach for his temperamental talent. Both Frost and Duval hit their tee shots on eighteen. As they exited the tee box, Blackmon turned to Duval and said, "Do you know how embarrassing it is going to be for you to walk up to the 18th green at the U.S. Open, in the final round, carrying your own bag?"

The words slowed everything down for Duval.

Low on resources in a family turned upside down, Duval grabbed onto his coach Blackmon like he was a dinghy in the middle of a shark-infested Atlantic. In the ensuing years, he would find solace in visiting his old coach at his home near the University of South Carolina. Duval would play with Blackmon's kids, Ashley, Jordan, and Tate, at their Columbia home. The Blackmons became an extended family once removed for Duval. He found solace in the time spent there and learned a little about devotion to both professional and spiritual life.

THE MAN BEHIND THE MASK

His senior year in 1993 was when he started getting criticized for slow play. Duval had never been one to contemplate a shot too long, but he kept losing his target. At the ACC Championships in Rocky Mount, North Carolina, he found a remedy—a pair of wraparound Oakley sunglasses. "Obviously, that time of year the pollen is really bad. The wind kept blowing the pollen in my eyes. I wore the glasses that week and I won, and I wore them the next week and won. I've worn them ever since," said Duval. Duval offered an aside to the image: "As unattractive as everybody felt they looked, they were extremely effective and they look pretty good to me," he said. They look so good to Duval's checkbook that what started with a sponsor for Georgia Tech's golf team has turned into a six-figure endorsement.

Blackmon remembers going to the NCAA Championship at the Champions Golf Club in Lexington, Kentucky, in 1993. His team finished second and Duval finished second individually, but it was the sunglasses that everyone was talking about. "People thought we were cocky because we had these sunglasses on. Harrison Frazar's mom was getting after me pretty good. I realized then that the sunglasses might not be the best thing for a wholesome image as far as David was concerned," said Blackmon.

When Duval graduated from Georgia Tech, *Golf Digest*'s Lisa Furlong went after another Duval physical trait. She nicknamed him Mr. Hair in the game of golf. Duval, not wanting to be tagged with a singular image, soon discarded the long blond hair for an image more in line with the top relief pitchers in the major leagues. "I pleaded with David to not go that route. But he cut his hair short, pulled his hat down, and while the glasses were good for him, I said, 'Let your game do the talking,'" said Blackmon.

So Duval, also a baseball junkie, adopted a look that was already a part of major league baseball. He had the scowl and the goatee of a relief pitcher and the goggles of a good right fielder. The look allowed Duval to shelter himself from the attention that goes along with being a single player with a game on the PGA Tour.

Clark Burroughs, a member of Jim Brown's Ohio State teams in the mid-'80s remembers playing golf with Duval a couple of times in 1989, Duval's streaky junior summer. "His dad (Bob Duval) was a pro near Jacksonville, and we got to play a couple of times. It was simple, really. He didn't like me, and I didn't like him," said Burroughs. Brown now calls the 1985 NCAA champion Burroughs "a little more than a free spirit." But it was Burroughs who caught Duval's attention on the Nike Tour.

Both players were in Mexico for the 1994 Mexico Open at Club Campestre. Burroughs, 32, recognized a talented 22-year-old whom he played a couple of rounds with in Jacksonville. Burroughs approached the usually unapproachable Duval and got to the business at hand. "I said I need a roommate. I asked him if he snored, and he said no, so we had a deal."

This was the beginning of the legend of Duval and Burroughs. Burroughs liked to call himself "the big rebel," as opposed to his sidekick, "the little rebel." Burroughs had won the NCAA championship at Ohio State in 1985. He was 10 years older than Duval, but not as mature. This made for a great relationship. From one week to the next, they would climb aboard Duval's dark-green Pathfinder in search of big money on the Nike Tour in which they both tagged about $5,000 a week. "That was our goal, $5,000 each week. If we came close to that, then it was a good week."

As roommates they both had a running bet. Whoever played best the week prior received a free room the following week at the expense of the higher finisher. "It went back and forth; he finished 8th on the money list, and I was 15th, so we each had our moments and the times when we needed to foot the bill," said Burroughs. Duval and Burroughs also socialized with Charlie Rymer, John Jumbo Elliott and Harry Rudolph. Playing cards, watching the Braves and just trying to win a paycheck each week was the totality of life in towns like Panama City, Cleveland, and Raleigh.

Burroughs remembers watching the stout version of Duval get out of a cart in Panama City and remarking, "You look like a freaking penguin. That's your new nickname." And so, Big Rebel and Little Rebel, aka the Penguin, were the male versions of Thelma and Louise in search of the big money on the Nike Tour.

Duval's Pathfinder was their chariot on the Nike Tour. Sometimes players on the Nike Tour steered clear of Duval and

Burroughs. "David had an edge to him, but I don't think enough people saw the other side of David. He was a super-nice guy; sure, he was completely focused. There is no question he did not let people get too close to him. But he had a keen sense of who wanted to hang out with him because he's David Duval and those who wanted to hang out with him because he was just a pretty nice guy," said Harry Rudolph. Rudolph was part of Duval's inner circle on the Nike circuit.

That first summer on the Nike Tour was a proving ground for Duval, who did not make the A squad (PGA Tour) in 1993. He miraculously finished in 11th place on the money list, less than $3,000 from getting his Tour card. He had only played in nine-events, which included two wins at the Wichita Open and the Nike Tour Championship. Two years later, when he played at the President's Cup he was kidded that he was the only one on the U.S. team without a win on Tour and asked how he would respond to the pressure. He said, "Well, actually I have two wins. I feel like the wins I had on the Nike Tour were exceptional wins."

TUESDAY AFTERNOONS
—THE MOODY BLUES

"We had some pretty good bets going on the putting green," said Burroughs. "Fives and tens, it was sometimes out of boredom, but it was great for our competitiveness." The week always started on Tuesday with Duval and Burroughs. This was the day they herded any prospective twosome into a practice-round wager. Burroughs and Duval sometimes challenged three other players in fivesomes on Tuesdays. It was their chance to make some extra money and create a Tournament feel early for the week. "We started winning fifties and hundreds, and it was soon after that nobody wanted to play us."

That's when the challenges turned from Tuesday afternoons on the course to Tuesday evenings in the hotel. Putting contests broke the monotony of minor league golf at Nike events. Duval and Burroughs would throw down a quarter and practice hitting putts to the coin. Then they would play some cards. It was a routine that each attacked out of boredom.

It was at the Residence Inn just outside of Cleveland, Ohio, in 1994, when Burroughs challenged Duval to a Tin Cup-like contest. Their room was located at the end of the hall on the second floor. Just beyond the door to their room was a balcony, which overlooked an adjacent empty field. The Big Rebel dared the Little Rebel to get the ball airborne from inside their room so that it would clear the railing and sail into the field.

Burroughs went first. He chose a 7-iron from his imaginary caddie and took aim. They checked the hallway for unsuspecting ice-cube fetchers. Burroughs stabbed his club in the carpet and the ball barely cleared the balcony on its way into the field about 160 yards. Then Duval took out a 3-iron. After another check to see if the hallway was clear, Duval's liner hit the top of the balcony and careened deep into the field. The indoor practice facility didn't help his game. He shot 75-78.

After winning twice on the Nike Tour in 1993 (Wichita Open and the Tour Championship), Duval was not used to events where he missed the cut. It was another introspective time for Duval, just another small losing streak. His Pathfinder hit the road to see girlfriend Julie MacArthur in Atlanta.

Two weeks later the two amigos teed it up in Raleigh, North Carolina, for the Carolina Classic. Duval tied for fifth at 8-under par, shooting a pair of 69s in the second and third rounds. His game was starting to spark. He would be returning to the Wichita Open in two weeks; a Tournament where he was the glamorous defending champion. A Tournament where he became the youngest ever (21 years, nine months) to win a Nike event.

His 1993 form was not there, however. He shot 73-74-147 and missed the cut. He earned $85 for the week. The previous summer he won $27,000 for the win. The Big Rebel (Burroughs), his roommate for the week, almost won the event, finishing a stroke behind Dennis Postlewait. Duval swallowed hard. He knew he didn't want to spend another year on the Nike Tour. At least Burroughs was going to pick up the hotel check at the Ozarks Open.

Duvall knew that if he wanted to be a member of the 1995 PGA Tour, he was going to have to finish strong. And he knew he was going to have to take care of business as the Nike Tour headed west. West was not an area of the country where Duval enjoyed a lot of success as a junior player. Other than his Boys' Junior win at El Cajon, California, he preferred the fairways on the east coast which was one reason he chose to attend Georgia Tech.

From the Ozarks Open in Missouri, then extending to the Tour Championship, just as he had done the summer of 1989, Duval began making birdies and didn't stop. He finished tied for third in the next two events (The Ozarks Open and the Texarkana Open). He collected $29,000 combined for two 14-under-par performances. He didn't stop there. In his next event he shot 65-74-69-66 for another 14-under-par performance at the University of New Mexico Course in Albuquerque. Two years earlier he had captained the Georgia Tech team in the NCAA Championships at the same course. The following week, Duval had his best overall finish in 1994 when he finished runner-up to Chris Perry in the Utah Classic in Provo. In four weeks, he earned $59,801 and had accumulated a season total over $105,000. With three events left, including the Tour Championship, he was in great position to earn exempt status on the PGA Tour. When he tapped in for 71 in the final round at the Tour Championship, his tie for sixth place was an afterthought. He earned his PGA Tour card.

"I knew he was the real deal," said Burroughs. "He never talked about being a four-time All-American, or his future goals. But I guarantee he knew them inside. His heart for golf is the size of the earth."

BE THE BALL

Battling head to head will soon become commonplace for many of the PGA Tour's 20-something players. They know each other's games. It was at the 1998 Tucson Open that Duval revealed his true character. He arrived in Tucson late—something about snowboarding on Mt. Baldy in Sun Valley. He opened with a 66 on Thursday, one stroke behind college rival Justin Leonard. Duval's second and third rounds (62-68) left him at 20-under, seven strokes ahead of Leonard to start play on Sunday. Unaccustomed to an avalanche lead on Sunday, especially a seven-stroke lead, the feisty Duval slipped as if he was back on his snowboard traversing Mt. Baldy, and Leonard clawed back. Standing on the 14th tee with a two-shot lead, Duval hooked his tee shot out-of-bounds.

"Things were going okay, and then I hit that shot," said Duval. Duval actually asked for another pellet from Mitch Knox and stuck with his driver to hit his third shot. "I know people said, 'uh, oh. What's he doing hitting a driver again?' I just knew there was one place it wasn't going to go the second time, and that was left," Duval laughed a sinister laugh.

Leonard and Duval battled in college and now the take was a little more. Fun? Fearless? Guts and game, they both have it. Leonard tried to make Tucson his first win of the 1998 season, but Leonard has carved a niche by coming from behind. To Leonard, an adrenaline rush is going 75 in his Porsche on the Dallas beltway, sinking a 30-footer and going birdie, par to win a major championship. Was this an adrenaline rush for Duval or just golf? "To actually fall back to being tied, and to pull it through, was just great," said Duval.

It must have been like making a jagged cut on a snowboard —Duval likes close calls. Leonard, always a tactician, became more learned, as he always does, and it made him a stronger player. A month later, Leonard charged from behind again and won the Players' Championship. These guys are good and they know it.

THE SUN ALSO RISES

The running of the Bulls in Pamplona or a Spanish bull-fight would make a good segment for ESPN2 and the X-Games. Frantic people running down the streets of Pamplona in death-defying chaos. Like the surge of concertgoers at a general admission concert or a bungee jump off the side of a bridge are all experiences in which the initial rush of exhilaration quickly skitters toward a mindful security. The millennium version would be snowboarding down a steep run, with little margin for error, trying to separate the importance of balance, navigating a course in quest for the end of the run.

Ernest Hemingway was captivated by a lot of things in his life—booze, women, the outdoors. Not a passive sort, Hemingway liked to live on the edge, and no better way to excite the senses than to run with the bulls. One summer during the event in Pamplona, he suffered a wound that required immediate attention. It was a wound that could have led to infection and much worse. Dr. George Saviers responded to the emergency, and Hemingway later wrote about the experience in the short story "The Dangerous Summer."

Saviers was in Spain with Hemingway. His practice was based in Sun Valley, Idaho, which quickly became a hideaway for Ernest and Mary Hemingway. They found the Sun Valley Lodge in Sun Valley, Idaho, to be a recreational and devotional refuge. The vistas and the serenity were inviting to the writer in his final years. A proven sportsman, Hemingway could go antelope hunting during the day and play poker at night. It was an area that stimulated the mind behind his literary craftsmanship, and it quickly became a getaway destination, which was part of his ultimate downfall. From 1953 to 61, Saviers was Hemingway's chief physician, and he was the first to recommend psychological counseling for the writer. The indignant Hemingway eventually lost a long battle over his own mind. The intellect that enlightened souls with graphic detail became brutal reality. He had become his own character of fiction. Not even the breathtaking beauty of Sun Valley pacified his soul enough to save him.

David Duval also found an isolation from the demanding rigors of the game of golf in the scenic beauty of Sun Valley, Idaho. Heading west on the Nike Tour gave him a sense of the scenic beauty of the mountainous regions. It was in 1996 that he first met two members of the Sun Valley community, Buck and JoAnn Levy. Duval met the retired couple in Sun Valley with then-caddie Jeff Weber and Julie MacArthur. The Levys call the location of their house "on campus." It is a place with a breathtaking view of the golf courses below and the vista of mountains and tributaries that run like veins through the frontier.

"This place is hassle-free. In five minutes we are at the grocery store, there's no crime, and we think it's bad we have three stoplights," said Buck Levy. Wally Huffman, who runs the Sun Valley company contacted 67-year-old Buck, and his wife, JoAnn, 10 years his junior, when he learned Duval was in town. He asked if they would mind spending some time showing a young couple around. Buck, a member of the 1956 Nordic Combined U.S. Winter Olympic team, and his wife, a longtime ski instructor, did the honors of introducing the raw terrain of the slopes to the threesome.

With JoAnn as their guide, Duval tested his love for skiing against the white-powdered elements of Sun Valley's most difficult runs. On many subsequent treks to Sun Valley, they ended up staying with Buck and JoAnn, sharing their appreciation for the land. As a loner, Duval found the solitude of Sun Valley and the blossoming friendship with the Levys an inspiring combination.

"My wife loves to cook, and I feel abused if my wife goes out," said Buck. "And I know David is not the kind of guy who likes to go out, sit at a bar and share stories. The relationship works for both of us."

Levy has an unbelievable memory for U.S. Open champions and the years and course on which they have won. Give him a simple year, for example, 1965, and Levy recites, "Gary Player at a course near St. Louis called Bellerive." He also holds a reverence for the works of Ernest Hemingway. A retired general practitioner, he shared a practice with George Saviers, the same George Saviers who served as physician and confidant to Hemingway. Duval is known for his ability to tackle tough reads like Ayn Rand, and has had several conversations with Levy about Hemingway. Duval has yet to consume some of the Hemingway manuscripts in the crowded (over 500 books) Levy library. He's too busy making the summer dangerous for others on the PGA Tour.

The Levys first began skiing and socializing with Duval in the winter of 1996. Since their first meeting, Duval's interest in skiing has waned in favor of snowboarding. Buck Levy said, "If you saw him snowboard, you would not think he's too worried about his golf game. You can't compare bad skiing conditions and the dangers, to an inclement round of golf."

Dangerous? Duval thinks hot coffee pots are dangerous. "It's kind of funny. With all the snowboarding . . . people seem to think I'm crazy to do it, I've never had any problems with that.

But trying to fix a cup of coffee, I tried to almost take myself out," said Duval. Like Hemingway, who compared the running of the bulls and bullfighting in Spain with a ritualistic art form, Duval is oozing red like a Spanish bullfighter. Only his are red numbers on PGA Tour leader boards.

"I think part of the fondness David has for this place is that there is never a discouraging word. Oh, and my wife is the nicest thing on the face of the earth." David and Buck play cards (gin) and talk. It's customary for them to engage in a friendly conversation about David's Tour statistics or discuss the voluminous articles and books written on fly-fishing. The two have truly forged a rare bond.

Buck Levy did not fully understand the celebrity side of Duval when they first met. It wasn't until he made it to the bottom of the mountain on a ski run with Duval that his status as an athlete became apparent. Even though Sun Valley attracts a wide range of celebrities like Arnold Schwarzenegger and Bruce Willis, Levy was surprised when Duval was spotted not long after they met. Wearing his ski goggles and a long duns-type ski cap that made him look like a court jester, Duval was so well camouflaged that Levy was sure he would go unnoticed among the throng of skiers. As they were getting on a lift to take them back up the mountain, another skier obviously saw through Duval's disguise and responded in hilarious fashion, "Hey, David Duval, I love you, dude." After all, outside of the ski cap, the man behind the mask wears the same kind of goggles to spin his craft on fairways.

Duval was so taken with his new friends, the Levys, that he invited them to spend April at the 1997 Masters. When Blackmon first met the Levys at the Masters, his first impression was, "These people were totally oblivious to the game of golf. But beneath their innocent exterior, the Levys knew much more than the game of golf. They knew the thoughtfulness of David Duval and the graciousness of Julie MacArthur. Buck Levy knows the game from a historical perspective and the swing from a physical science perspective. All they knew was that this nice young man invited them to a golf Tournament. Before the 1997 Masters, Buck Levy mostly remembers golf by the way Nicklaus battled Palmer at the 1962 U.S. Open. They had nothing else to do, so they accepted the spring invitation. Duval took a fancy to the couple, and enjoyed their friendship and the calm it provided at Augusta. In 1998, the fancy of Augusta had evolved into a flame being carried by the hottest player in the game.

Duval took aim at Augusta in 1998. But it was Fred Couples who was the story through three rounds. The 1992 champion was at 6 under, playing smart golf. Then, like most Sunday back nines at Augusta, the chase was on. Duval quickly became the chased. Couples' approach shot at 9 spun off the green, and he made bogey. Duval was riding his best round of the Tournament. He made a string of six birdies starting at 7. When he tapped in for birdie on 15, he suddenly had a three-stroke lead. Until he hit his worst shot of the day. He pushed a 6-iron on the par-3 16th. Unable to stop a hard-breaking right-to-left slider off the now-famous Davis Love hill, Duval settled for a bogey. This left him in great position, until O'Meara rolled in his climactic putt on 18.

Duval watched the putt on a color monitor in the Jones Cabin. In the press room he was despondent, answering tough questions pointing to his low round. Duval knew inside that his effort wasn't a Scott Hoch finish at the Masters. After all, he had the best round (67) on Sunday. Afterward, he found a shoulder by calling Blackmon, who was returning from a trip with the South Carolina golf team at Auburn. Duval was headed to play in a Hootie and the Blowfish fund-raiser on Monday with his former coach.

"I could barely hear him, his voice was so low," said Blackmon. Blackmon pulled Duval up like he had done at Georgia Tech and said, "You better get over it. You did everything you needed to do to win that golf Tournament. You birdied the holes on Sunday that guys just don't birdie. You just got beat." David responded to his coach with the brashness of a champion, "There was never a doubt in my mind that I was going to win that golf Tournament."

When Duval showed up at Blackmon's house in South Carolina, Blackmon continued his advice to his young lion. David's motto has always been: "It's not who gets there the quickest, it's who gets there and stays there the longest. Build on the foundation of the Masters." Duval knew exactly what Blackmon meant. Part of the reason Duval went to Georgia Tech was the forethought that he would be on the college team that got to visit Augusta National. That's just the way Bobby Jones (Georgia Tech '22) wanted it. Jones, who won golf's grand slam in 1930, when he captured the U.S. Amateur, the U.S. Open, the British Open and the British Amateur, was a young icon, just like Duval, only Jones retired from the game at the age of 28. Duval was building "the foundation."

The Tuesday after the Masters, Duval showed up in Blackmons' kitchen, bag packed, shorts, a Titleist hat and flip-flops, ready for a drive home to Florida. "I'm not stopping until I get home," said Duval. Blackmon knew the pain of Augusta was still with the rising star. Blackmon thought to himself, "How do you tell a player like David it's all about believing in the foundation?"

Only if Mark O'Meara had not made that putt. The legendary Bobby Jones would have been so proud of the meeting at Butler Cabin. Two Georgia Tech players meeting in Butler Cabin at Augusta. Duval, the champion, wearing the green jacket and Matt Kuchar the low amateur. While Duval narrowly missed destiny, Georgia Tech sophomore Matt Kuchar won the event's Mr. Congeniality contest in 1998. The 19-year-old U.S. Amateur Champion charmed the galleries and offered a glimpse of what could be future battles between two Yellow Jackets.

Kuchar's debut at Augusta was scintillating. He grooved his "bumblebee"-logoed golf ball around Augusta, not like a wide-eyed college kid, but like an experienced veteran. And while the flight of Kuchar's golf ball earned him a return invitation with a top 24 finish (t-21), it was the trajectory of his smile that won admiration. "My smile may be a bit of an embarrassment," he said. "I just can't believe this many people are watching me play golf." Kuchar shot a third-round 68 and finished at even-par 288.

"The best feeling all week was the ovation we got when we teed off on 1," said Kuchar. He was paired with defending champion Tiger Woods. Kuchar also followed Woods in the winner's circle, since Woods won the U.S. Amateur from 1994 to 1996.

It was the Tiger and the Yellow Jacket in search of the green jacket. If this were a jungle, Kuchar would not have had a chance. Instead, he exceeded everyone's expectations, finishing ahead of such players as Davis Love III, John Daly and Lee Janzen. Kuchar's play and the antics of his dad carrying his bag would bedevil Justin Leonard and other players in the year's majors. PGA Tour players did not care to see a player like Kuchar skip school and nudge them off cut lines, just like when Mickelson turned pro after his Northern Telecom win as an amateur.

Despite Kuchar's play at Augusta and at The Olympic Club (1998 U.S. Open), where he tied for 14th, he admits to not being the best player at Georgia Tech.

Bryce Molder spent most of the 1999 season as the No. 1-ranked player in the country. He won the 1998 Jack Nicklaus award as a freshman. While Kuchar smiles, Molder smolders birdies on the competition. Heading into the 1999 NCAA Tournament, Molder, had a power rating of 69.20, second only to Joel Kribel of Stanford (68.85). Kuchar was ranked 24th (70.84).

Georgia Tech was faced with NCAA sanctions after a recent Mastercard ad in *Golf Digest* featured Kuchar.

Puggy Blackmon now refers to Georgia Tech's golf team in past tense, as if it were Oklahoma State and not the same program that he brought into prominence when he took over in 1981. Georgia Tech had not won a golf Tournament the 10 years prior to his arrival. He took on the challenge of creating a golf school at one of the most urban settings in America, Atlanta. Atlanta was a megalopolis that didn't have a golf course on campus. Blackmon resurrected the program by relying on the AJGA tip sheets (Tournament results). The Yellow Jackets have been ranked nationally consistently since 1985. Blackmon left Georgia Tech in 1995 for South Carolina. Duval had started to consider relocation to Atlanta before Blackmon bolted.

Blackmon admitted, "I had to explain to David that he was so invigorating to be around. I told all my players. You guys go here four years and then you leave. I don't go with you guys. When I left Georgia Tech, I was really burned out, and I lost a lot of interest. My relationship with David was a part of all that."

Clark Burroughs remembers the impact of the South Carolina move. "David really thought he might wear a Cocks hat, and there was some animosity toward the school when Puggy left." Bruce Heppler took over at Georgia Tech for Blackmon. Heppler served as an assistant at Oklahoma State for four years prior to replacing Blackmon. Heppler recruited three AJGA All-Americans from Florida—Sal Spallone, Jeremy Anderson, and Matt Kuchar—the summer he was hired for the Atlanta-based school.

"I really thought Anderson was the one player I was going to get," said Heppler. Kuchar ended up being the only player of the three whom he landed. And with Kuchar, Heppler started the program where Blackmon left off. The new regime under Heppler has not shown an interest in bridging the past with the team's future. As with a lot of NCAA Division I programs, a new coach and players cultivate a new set of objectives. Heppler and Blackmon view the Yellow Jacket past in a different perspective.

AFTER THE STREAK

Duval's 1998 campaign had started where it had left off in 1997. He was in the hunt at the season-opening Mercedes Championship at La Costa. After the third round, he was one stroke off the lead. Because of Friday showers, the Tournament committee allowed the players to play winter rules. Being able to lift-clean-and-place the ball leveled the field. After three rounds, Duval was one stroke back; John Cook and Nick Price were two back. Duval was again chasing Phil Mickelson, his boyhood and college nemesis, only this time it was on the PGA Tour.

Giving Mickelson the ability to touch the golf ball and place it was like giving Reggie Miller time to set his feet and take aim behind the 3-point arc. Mickelson's final-round 68 edged the Isleworth, Florida, duo of Mark O'Meara and Tiger Woods, who both finished with 64s. Duval idled in with a 73 and a top-10 finish (6th). A week later at the Bob Hope Chrysler Classic, Duval recorded five rounds in the 60s (65-67-68-67-68) to finish tied for fourth.

His quick 1998 was almost identical to what he accomplished in 1999. Before the season started, at the Mercedes Championship, he quantified his position as a player coming of age on the PGA Tour: "I think I am content with where I am, what I'm doing, and with who I am. I am content with my hobbies. I think just generally it all plays a part." Laid back? He referenced his duck-hooked driver at Tucson, a Tournament he won in 1998, as one that he "got a kick out of." Duval stood up on the next tee at Tucson and pulled the driver out again. In 1999, he pulled his game out from the first round in Maui and put the pedal to the metal with a 26-under-par and a nine-shot (277 total) win over the field at the Kapalua Plantation Course.

Buck Levy references Hemingway, just as he references Duval's earnings, to the penny. He also has memorized weekly statistical marks. There is a shared sense of respect between Levy and Duval. Levy argues categorically that Duval's 1998 was the best statistical performance by any PGA Tour player ever, from greens in regulations to putts to average driving distance. Levy has a penchant for numbers, and he said, "Duval's numbers don't lie. I tried to tell Tim Rosaforte last year that his numbers were the best ever." Buck Levy holds Duval's numbers in high esteem as he offers an assessment of the lad: "David Duval is a very bright person. He's laconic. There is no need to tell him how smart he really is."

Duval and Julie MacArthur met up with the Levys after the win at the Mercedes earlier in 1999. Like Buck's friendly ribbings of Duval's year-to-date earnings, he really wanted to discuss a theory he had about David's game. The two were playing a game of gin, when he thought about mentioning a statistical analysis he had done. Levy backed off the thought, thinking it might be placing a burden on the young player's shoulders. Then, it sort of spilled out of his mouth. I told him, "I want to show you a little math I've done. With the short layouts at some of the Tour stops...with the number of par fives you can hit in two and the amount of sand wedges you will be hitting into par fours, you gain a huge statistical advantage." If you take the probability that he will shoot, say, 3.8 on the par fours, add up all the fractions. I told him he was going to shoot in the 50s.

Duval was waiting to accept the championship trophy at the Bob Hope after shooting 59 when he turned to Julie and said, "Buck said I was going to shoot in the 50s."

In this case, Hemingway's prophecy, "You lose it if you talk about it," was far from the truth. The truth was that Buck Levy called the 59 at the Bob Hope. Levy did not go so far as to say it would happen at the Bob Hope, but his hunch was that it would happen sooner rather than later. Another funny coincidence with Buck and JoAnn Levy is that the last four digits of their phone number are 5959. They insist they have had the phone number for a long time.

Numbers usually don't lie, but as Duval made the dogleg into 1999, he may have wondered how he could have won four times in 1998, finished second at the Masters, and claimed 12 top-10 finishes and still was not holding the Jack Nicklaus Award as the Player of the Year.

Duval's golf ball was giving marketing giants at Nike in Beaverton, Oregon, fits. One year earlier, Tigermania had hit the mainstream. And now the smooth-swinging Duuvy was creating his own niche. He gets more excited about extreme skiing than reaching a par-5 in two. He had won the Houston Open like Tiger dusted the field at Augusta in 1997???. It was a brilliant display of golf. Since Tiger's benchmark win for the ages to the Houston Open in 1998, Duval had won five times to a single event for Tiger. Check the tale of the tape, and Duval has had nine top 10s during the same period to Tiger's seven. Role reversal or the ebb and flow of life on the PGA Tour. Time will reveal everything, even their swing thoughts.

"WHEN YOU COMING HOME DAD?" "I DON'T KNOW WHEN. WE'LL GET TOGETHER THEN." —HARRY CHAPIN

The kid said to Dad on the eve of their coinciding Florida Tournaments, "You are going to think about winning...When you think about it, embrace it; recognize what you're doing and push it aside." Bob Duval had never won before on the Senior

PGA Tour. His son had bagged nine events. The final rounds at the TPC Sawgrass and the Moors Golf Club unfolded like a made-for-television drama.

The older Duval fired a final-round 71 and held off renaissance man Bruce Fleisher to claim the Emerald Coast Classic. Little Duval captured the Players' Championship just down the street from their hometown course Timuquana, making them the first father-son duo to ever win on the same weekend. Not Ray and Robert Floyd, Al and Brent Geiberger. Not Dave Stockton and Dave Stockton Jr. Not Jack and Gary Nicklaus. The Duvals? The Duvals get results. For other families, golf has been a pastime. For the Duvals, it has been an odyssey. Bob Duval knew the elements of the golf swing, but the elements of family was something he and David both had a difficult time understanding.

Bob Duval used to be a scorer in the tent on 18 at the Players Championship. Not this year. David used to get his dad a hat so the players could autograph it after their round. David was signing the autographs in 1999.

David remembers watching Seve Ballesteros and José Maria Olazabal practice at the 6th green, playing shots that would allow them an opportunity to get the ball up and down. He remembers standing behind the gallery ropes on the range, watching Jack Nicklaus, Ray Floyd, Tom Kite play practice shot after practice shot—watching carefully as they sent white flares into the air. Then, there was the year Bernhard Langer brought a bagful of drivers to the range. One by one he tried them out.

In 1993, he left Atlanta and the Georgia Tech campus to watch Nick Price win the title. Bernhard Langer was within striking distance when Price made his way to the 17th, the island green. Ever since the Players Championship began in 1977, it seemed the island green played a factor in the outcome. He recalls Price's shot as if he were watching it like everyone else that year—from the gallery.

Duval said, "He walked up there; grabbed his club, stood out over the ball and hit it. He just never gave himself a chance to think about anything other than hitting it up there close."

Back then, the junior version of Duval was on the outside looking in on the great players. Now he was on the inside looking out. He rehearsed in his mind the moment when he could compete at the TPC Sawgrass. What it would mean and how it would feel if he could somehow grow up and play inside the ropes.

"Obviously, I dreamt about it. But, I am not going to tell you I knew I was going to come here and win the golf Tournament," said Duval. His dad sipped champagne while he watched Justin Leonard present his son with the trophy.

Born and raised in Jacksonville, David Duval spent 15 years watching players compete at the TPC Sawgrass. One year he was asked to be a marker on Saturday. He was paired with Joey Sindelar. After five holes, Scott Hoch dropped out with a bad back. Norman was then paired with Sindelar, and his first-ever opportunity to play in the Tournament was dashed. "I was one-under through five," said Duval.

Duval was the first alternate at the Players Championship when he was 18, and now, in 1999, he had emerged as the No. 1 player in the world. "It is nice to be ranked No. 1, but it is not a concern of mine. I had that stretch when I won nine events." And with the Players Championship, Duval was like a snowball at Sun Valley, Idaho, heading south. Since October 19, 1997, Duval has been either one or two in the world rankings.

Sun Valley affords Duval an opportunity to be himself. When he gets there, it's like a distance runner who breaks through the wall where pain meets exhaustion and the mental capacity to control. "It is when David extends his mind outside of golf that he really enjoys. He gets more excited about fishing and extreme skiing than anything else," said Blackmon.

The photo sessions, the interviews, his agent Charley Moore's insistence that he do the things to create an image for the business side of the sport really is not Duuvy's choice. It comes with the territory of being heralded as the next Nicklaus that he can do without.

At the 1999 Houston Open, Duval, an avid baseball fan, threw out the first pitch at a Houston Astros game. At Westchester he found time to take batting practice before a Mets-Marlins game.

Duval also went to school with a pretty good baseball player at Georgia Tech—Nomar Garciaparra. In 1997, while Duval was breaking through in Williamsburg, the Red Sox shortstop was also breaking through. Both players were doing incredible things with a white ball. It was Garciaparra's first summer at Fenway Park when he went on a Duval-like tear, batting .306 with 30 homers, 98 RBIs, and 122 runs. The Red Sox shortstop was named the American League Rookie of the Year. Duval was named Mr. October (Player of the Month) on the PGA Tour.

Duval had won over a million dollars on Tour by March of 1998, which is when Nomar signed a $23.25 million, five-year deal with Boston. Two years later, both Georgia Tech products are warranting DiMaggio and Nicklaus comparisons. Both are streak-driven professional athletes.

As Duval began to emerge on the fairways of the PGA Tour, ESPN's John Barrett noticed him as an outdoorsman. Barrett's celebrity fishing show has offered the likes of Bobby Knight—even Johnny Miller took part in "fly-fishing the world" with Barrett. In June of 1998, Barrett asked Duval to fish "The Big Hole" in Montana, a tributary that serves the Yellowstone River. Duval asked his friend Buck Levy to make the trip together as a part of the expedition. A noted fisherman, Barrett bragged about his ability to cast a long line. Although Duval was an avid fisherman, his fishing muscles were not like his golf muscles. He and Levy deferred to the expert as they set their flies for a morning Tour. Levy and Duval usually head to the Wood River and Silver Creek near Sun Valley, so fishing the Big Hole was a new stream and a new experience.

Levy tried to stay out of Barrett's way so the ESPN film crew would be able to capture the expert, Barrett, schooling the novice, Duval, on the art of fly-fishing. Levy said, "David's very determined to become a very adept fly-fisherman." This was his chance to see Barrett explain the craft in "casting a long line." As Barrett let out the line to set his rod into a whip-like casting motion, Levy sensed there might be trouble. Duval, unawares, took notice of the motion, equating it to teeing up a driver on hole number eight at Pinehurst No. 2 and letting the shaft out. Barrett cracked his rod like a whip with a forward thrust. The velocity was supposed to impress. Instead of the tiny feather-light fly finding the waters, it found the flesh in the back of Duval's neck.

Levy, who was considered somewhat of a space liability on the trip, was urged out of retirement. He happened to have some hemostats with him, and he extracted the fly from just below Duval's hairline in the back of his neck.

Duval and Levy enjoyed sojourns to the Bayou for redfish after Duval's win in Atlanta, and they enjoy the "catch and release" streams that carve through nature in Sun Valley. Buck Levy said, "David doesn't want to be 45 and say, 'I' wish I'd done a lot of things'. I think it's wonderful to seize the opportunity."

Duval knows a lot about seizing an opportunity. From his jab at the AJGA in 1989 to his success on the PGA Tour in 1999, he has measured his stoic greatness one spike print at a time. Tiger Woods was a lottery pick, Mickelson leapfrogged the Nike Tour and Q-school with a PGA win as an amateur. Duval earned his stripes. He failed to make it on Tour at the 1993 Q-school, and it has made him appreciate the opportunity he's earned.

For Duval, the emotion inside will always be more important than the adulation of the gallery. His sense of purpose has been built by an understanding that one day he might be standing on top of the world, and the next day it might not be there. His longevity in the game will likely be shorter than some of the other players on the PGA Tour. Duval knows the importance of living in the moment, spending more time in Sun Valley. He learned from his father on the range at Timuquana that the game cannot be perfected, and it cannot be allowed to consume the mental capacity; it must be kept in perspective. Blackmon and Levy have given David Duval a sense of settled confidence. More important, Duval knows the sun also rises away from the golf course.

TO THE WOODS AND BACK

Chris Haack was pacing back and forth like an expectant father. The AJGA's first-ever Canon Cup at Lake Nona Golf Club in Orlando was commencing. Players for both teams were arriving at the host hotel with aplomb. For Haack, the captain of the West team, the chatter around the hotel was starting to become irritating. He heard unexpected comments regarding his selection of a 14-year-old from California. Even the kids were starting to reinforce what he feared most. "They were saying things like, 'When's the little kid going to get here? Why did you pick Tig?',", Haack said.

An 18-year-old, Trip Kuehne, remembers watching the nervous captain summon idle feedback on his selection. It did not come from Kuehne, one of Tiger's teammates for the West team. Kuehne shared the pervading sentiment: with guys getting ready to head to the best golf schools in the nation, why did Haack pick a 14-year-old kid like Tiger Woods?

The mixed-team, Ryder Cup-like format was designed to showcase the best 15- to 18-year-old boys and girls in the nation.

The format was new, but sponsor Canon wanted to feature the next college all-stars. Haack, being the calculating strategist, went off the board and selected a little kid the way David Stern goes to the podium to announce the next high school star jumping the college game for the NBA. Haack wanted to look like Kevin McHale selecting Kevin Garnett. He didn't want a bust.

Stephen Hamblin, captain of the East, joked with Haack, "Why don't you just give us the Canon Cup. You don't know what you're doing." Haack was hard-pressed to find anyone that supported his pick.

"Tiger Woods is a player, you'll see," he muttered. Haack knew that Woods had won the "Big I" Insurance Classic, and that alone was confirmation that Woods could play. He also finished second in the PGA Junior, another non-AJGA event, but a premier kids' tournament.

It was easy to irritate Haack. He was the incessant prankster among the members of the AJGA staff, but he was not a gracious recipient of criticism. He was like a big brother to many of the AJGA players, including Woods. Haack never backed down from verbal jabbing, and with his Craig Stadler-type build, robust opinions were the norm. "I am a pretty bold guy, but I was really unprepared for that kind of criticism, and I was worried that Tiger might not be ready for it," remembers Haack.

Haack's pacing intensified to the point that he was now chatting with parents and players, trying to take his mind off what he thought could be disaster before the first ball was struck at Lake Nona. Another thought entered Haack's mind. It was the first tournament in which Tiger's father, Earl, stayed at home and let his son sojourn across America for the mixed-team, end-of-the season event. Maybe Woods was going to be homesick, or even intimidated by the older players in Orlando.

Haack remembers Woods was one of the last players to enter the hotel lobby. Without hesitation, Haack walked up to the bag-toting, travel-weary youngster and offered his hand. Haack remembers a short introduction followed by an invitation for a practice round. Haack's harpooned conscience needed to get his young player on the course to check out his game.

At the age of 14, Tiger's legend had made its way through the communication channels of the junior golf circuit in a hurry, but Haack wanted to witness Tiger's game for himself. He had not seen Tiger play in any events, and he wanted to confirm his hunch. By the eighth hole of the practice round, Haack's mind was at ease. He knew Tiger's selection was warranted. His game had all the distance of the older boys in the field, and his short game was what kids were calling "no fear."

Haack decided to hit a 3-wood on No. 9. Haack, a former AJGA player in the days of Willie Wood and Andrew Magee, slammed his tee shot to the base of the fairway from the elevated tee. Tiger took out his driver and sent the ball on a long, high trajectory. When they got to their balls, Haack had noticed what every Joe six-pack likes to witness when he's playing with a ringer. "I guess I got you there," he whispered to the embarrassed Woods.

Haack wanted to build a relationship with Woods, and this was his opportunity. "That might have been the world's greatest 3-wood," Haack chided. Haack knew the mixed match-play format over the next three days would create a little animosity among the brat-pack juniors. East versus West was going to soon become a Mississippi River—like conquering line descending on the best junior golfers (boys and girls) in the nation. He jokingly wanted to test the mental capacity of his young player. Even at a young age, Tiger was used to getting ribbed. He shrugged it off. Next shot.

The East went on to beat the West 38-18 in the 1990 Canon Cup. But it wasn't the fault of the 14-year-old from Cypress, California. Woods demonstrated the drive he had to succeed in match play. In the event's final match, Woods played Daniel Stone. Stone, from St. Petersburg, Florida, was 1 up through three. On the short par-four 4th hole, Stone knocked his approach shot six inches from the cup for a certain birdie. Woods took a little longer than usual over his short-iron approach into the green. The AJGA's Pete Ripa recalls Woods' high finish on his approach shot. "He held that club in his finish while the ball hit the green. I said to myself, this is a pretty composed kid." Woods' shot hit the green and rolled in the cup for an eagle two. Instead of Stone being 2-up after four, the match was now even. Woods went on to beat Stone 2 and 1.

Woods represented the West on the Canon Cup team from 1991 to 1993. Haack did not let people forget his historic choice in 1990. "A 14-year-old wasn't supposed to beat an 18-year-old, no matter how good he was. In that tournament, Tiger said hello, golf world, and the legend started to grow," said Kuehne. Kuehne got to know Woods away from the course at the Canon Cup. He added, "At that tournament, I learned that Tiger Woods didn't just want to play golf, he was a competitor who wanted to dominate, especially in match play."

AUGUSTA NATIONAL (NINE YEARS LATER)

Haack caddied for Willie Wood for the par-3 tournament at the Masters in 1999. Wood, because of his last name, was alphabetically linked to Tiger Woods at a lot of tournaments, whether it was on the driving range, in the men's locker room or simply by confused neophyte gallery members looking at pairings sheets. On Wednesday, Wood and Woods were situated next to each other on the range. And Haack, disguised in Masters caddie whites, happened to be the looper for Willie Wood. Wood was the dominant player in junior golf in the late 1970s. Just over five feet tall, he still looks the part of a junior golfer. Wood has been a study in perseverance on the PGA Tour since his All-American days at Oklahoma State in the early 1980s.

Two years after Tiger's record-setting triumph at Augusta, the old Canon Cup captain, Haack, was standing in close proximity to the tiger cub he had selected nine years earlier in 1990. Woods, the king of junior golf in the 1990s, was next to the smaller, but older king of junior golf in the late 1970s, Wood. Haack, never one to shy away from an opportunity, stopped Wood from hitting his 7-iron to showcase a confrontation he had hoped would someday come.

Haack stopped Wood from hitting balls. He said, "Hey Willie, ask Tiger what's the greatest 3-wood he's ever seen." Wood, a natural prankster in the Haack mode, walked to the next range station well within earshot of Woods and announced, "Hey Tiger, what's the world's greatest 3-wood you've ever seen." Woods decoded the verbal message and continued hitting range balls. Wood, not knowing if the Tiger had heard him, jabbed again, "Tiger, who hit the greatest 3-wood of all time?" Woods spun around to see his old captain standing in his caddie whites. Tiger fired back with a smile, "Get the hell outta here, Haack."

Woods knew exactly what Haack was referring to with his question. The legendary 3-wood at the 9th hole at Lake Nona was beginning to haunt him. He knew Haack would never let go of that moment, and he wanted it that way. Just down the range from Woods was Hank Kuehne. Kuehne had his brother Trip caddying for him. Haack didn't realize it at the time, but it was like a reunion for the 1990 West Canon Cup team. Kuehne, known for his 1998 U.S. Amateur win and tee-ball velocity, was sending 3-wood shots, one at a time, into the net guarding Washington Street.

Woods has admitted to being outdistanced by Kuehne. But a combination of Kuehne missiles and good-natured barbs from Haack had begun to stoke Tiger's furnace. His competitive side was lit like a fuse. He could not passively sit and accept being upstaged by Kuehne and the glorified 3-wood-hitting Masters caddie and former Canon Cup captain. He heard another gallery-like quip from Haack. "Tiger, show me something." Tiger grabbed his 3-wood and pegged a terrified Augusta range ball. As Woods sent the shot into orbit, a certain reverence returned to the Augusta range.

Haack, was three years removed from the AJGA in 1999. He was in the midst of his third season as the golf coach at the University of Georgia. From his early days working with Mike Bentley and the AJGA to Augusta National, Haack had watched the kids with games rise through the ranks of amateur and college golf—then on the PGA Tour. In three years, he built a national championship team at Georgia, plucking the most talented AJGA players in the nation for his squad. The Bulldogs won the NCAA championship in 1999, two months after his reunion with Tiger.

The Augusta range reunion also marked a change in the way Tiger Woods attacked a golf course. Until recently, Woods awed galleries with the length of his 3-wood. Now he is wowing galleries and finds folly with the touch of his 3-wood—around the greens. He used the 3-wood several times around the greens at the U.S. Open at Pinehurst. Woods learned both on and off the course how to harness the energy of his golf game and his emotions. Some of what he learned was from an old teammate from the 1990 Canon Cup team, Trip Kuehne. Four years older than Woods, Kuehne helped him understand the future: "I tried to make it easier for him. I realized at that tournament that Tiger wanted to be the number-one player in the world, win major tournaments and make lots of money."

Kuehne saw the determination and the level of study in the young version of Woods. "He would tell me the importance of improving and what I thought about the mental aspect of the game," recalled Kuehne. The two formed a friendship that would be tested four years later.

Call it just plain fate. Woods and Kuehne were in different brackets of the 1994 U.S. Amateur at TPC Sawgrass in Ponte Vedra, Florida. Woods shot an opening-round 65 over the rain-soaked layout. The rain had reduced the course to a long-ball-striker's alley. Mother nature had chiseled the field to the big hitters. This included both Woods and Kuehne.

The finals pairings featured friends. But the friendship was put aside for 36 holes.

Kuehne opened the match by birdieing seven of the first 13 holes. He took a commanding 5-up lead after the first 18 and was still 4-up with ten holes to play. He stepped on to the par-5 9th tee, charged by a surge of adrenaline. "I smoked a drive on 9 and was 20 yards farther than I have ever been on that hole," said Kuehne. Woods, even slighter in build than the slender Kuehne, was derailed by his driver all day. He admitted, "At the time I did not know where it was going."

On the 9th he put his drive behind Kuehne, but it was playable. Kuehne, being farther down the fairway than he had been all week, was met with indecision. He finally hit a 4-iron and he called it, "The worst 4-iron I've ever hit in competition." His father remembers the shot in a similar context: "It was basically a momentum buster." The shot ended up short of the green in a bunker. He bogeyed the 9th, and Woods won the hole with a par. "As I look back, that is the one shot I want back," said Kuehne.

Woods blocked his tee shot on 10 into the woods on the right. Somehow he managed par. Kuehne, reeling from the bogey on 9, made another bogey. Woods seized the momentum on 11 and made birdie. In three short holes, Kuehne's lead was whittled to 1-up with seven to play. The two players matched strides until the 16th, where Woods made a birdie and Kuehne made par. The match was even, but Kuehne knew he maxed out on birdies with two difficult holes to play.

Looking back, Kuehne said, "I was definitely playing the best golf of my life, but I felt like I used up all my birdies. In a day when you're playing 36 holes, you're only going to have so many. And I had all of mine early," said Kuehne. Kuehne and Woods grew up in junior golf, they had shared pickup basketball games in the Kuehne's backyard. They talked about life more than they talked about golf, and now, with two holes to play in the biggest amateur event ever, there had to be a winner.

Woods took dead aim at the pin at the island green 17th. His shot was on line, but flirted with the water. It came up short, but it was on the fringe, and most important it was dry. Woods watched as Kuehne lagged a putt close to the hole. Woods chose to putt the ball. He knew the putt was going to take a dive to the left about halfway to the hole. He stroked the putt on his imaginary line, and as it started turning left, Woods started walking left. As the ball dove into the hole, the game of golf suddenly changed. The straw-hatted Woods shot his right arm in upper-cut fashion to stake claim to his first U.S. Amateur. It will likely be one of the shots that shape his career.

The 1-up lead was all he needed. He battled back on the back nine at the TPC at Sawgrass. He couldn't find any fairway on the back nine in the U.S. Amateur, and he somehow cut the margin down to size. He had erased the largest deficit ever in a U.S. Amateur. This was fairy-tale stuff. Woods won the anticlimactic 18th but Kuehne knew he hadn't lost the U.S. Amateur.

Woods claimed the victory, his first of three straight runs in the tournament.

After losing to Tim Herron at the 1992 U.S. Amateur and making it to the round of 32 in 1993, he had emerged from out of the "Woods" at Sawgrass. "Tiger Woods won the trophy that day, and he was the U.S. Amateur Champion, but I won just as much as he did," said Kuehne.

Woods tried to collect his thoughts after his first major amateur win. At 18 years, seven months, and 29 days, he was the youngest champion ever in tournament history, dating back to 1895. He thanked his father, mother, and was grateful for just the opportunity to play the game. He also thanked Kuehne, who pushed him to his biggest win of his young career.

The golfing world would witness Woods holding the Havemeyer trophy two more times. Some impressive names grace the Havemeyer Trophy: Gene Littler, Jack Nicklaus, Arnold Palmer, Mark O'Meara and a trio of young champions named Mickelson (1990), Leonard (1993) and now Woods (1994).

In little over a year's time, Woods accepted a scholarship to play golf at Stanford, won the U.S. Amateur, Western Amateur, and Pacific Northwest Amateur, and played in three PGA Tour events (Nissan Los Angeles Open, Honda Classic and the Byron Nelson Classic).

BACK FROM THE WOODS

When Woods won the Memorial Tournament in 1999, his mind escaped to another major tournament when he couldn't seem to find fairways and greens. "The short-game shots, I've always loved hitting those shots," Woods said after the tournament. He added, "I love the challenge of chipping and putting or scrambling. That's the way I grew up. I was so wild off the tee that I had to do that. If you watched my first U.S. Amateur that I won at Sawgrass, I never hit a fairway on the back nine."

Woods doesn't have to remind anyone of the way he used to play. His last name was where his ball would often land. And so he cultivated a short game to go with the power. He has hit a new stride in the development of his game. In less than a decade, Woods has taken his full-throttle approach and slowly backed off.

"I've improved both mentally and physically," he said. "I think what people see is the physical changes because that's more apparent. But I've really improved on my management skills. Like learning more shots and how to position golf balls around a golf course and make the most of it when you don't have it." Woods learned early the steamroll approach to cognitive golf. On every hole, every swing, his father would encourage him to evaluate the swing process and the results.

"SOMETIMES YOU CAN'T BELIEVE WHAT YOU SEE, YOU HAVE TO BELIEVE WHAT YOU FEEL." —MORRIE SCHWARTZ IN *Tuesdays with Morrie* BY MITCH ALBOM

Woods used a dazzling display of short-game creativity and precision to win at Muirfield. After chili-dipping a wedge shot from the deep rough behind the 14th green, Woods was giving Vijay Singh reason to salivate over a potential momentum swing. That's when Woods' next chip burrowed in the cup for par. Somehow, Woods reversed his strengths at Jack's course. His short game became the signature of his win.

After he made the chip of the tournament, he sauntered to the 15th tee and sat on a bench with David Duval. This was supposed to be the first day in the beginning of the mano y mano challenge between the game's best. No. 1 versus No. 2. Instead, Duval sat on the bench, sullen because of his inability to make a run at the surging Woods. The two players knew to expect a comparison based on the world rankings. What are the media to do? The two best players in the world, sitting on a bench at Jack Nicklaus' Muirfield Village, and no time for an arm-wrestling contest. Time to check where the game is heading.

Nicklaus has made a habit of acknowledging performance, and Woods' final round just outside of Columbus awed even the Golden Bear.

"His short game was unbelievable. Most players at 23 don't have an imagination like that," said Nicklaus at the Memorial. He said, "The game is changed because of these young players, no doubt about it."

CARDINAL VIRTUES

Part of the Tiger Woods story involves an inner drive. Another part also involves a man named Phil Knight. Knight, CEO of the Nike empire, has been called the most influential man in sports. In the early 1960s he was a graduate student at Stanford University's School of Business. A professor named Frank Shallenberger asked Knight to write a paper about small business. Knight was a track-and-field junkie. He loved the sport for its brevity and was inspired by the potential for a better track shoe. An average runner at Oregon, Knight still had an Olympic cauldron full of desire to see the sport evolve. At the time, a company called Adidas was making shoes that appealed to everyone from serious runners to kids looking for a new fad. Knight knew there was room in the market for another player, so his short-paper topic became an obsession.

After graduating from Stanford in 1962, Knight took a flight to Japan to secure a distribution channel in America. He was chasing a dream of starting his own sneaker company. He was oblivious to it then, but 1962 was the "Year of the Tiger."

The irony was actually layers deep. Knight was en route to Onitsuka Co., Ltd. They made an imitation of the more popular Adidas shoe, and the only thing they lacked were distribution channels. After landing in Japan, Knight descended on the headquarters of the Onitsuka Company. The company's brand name was Tiger. The Onitsuka Company is known today as ASICS TIGER Corporation in America; its international headquarters is still in Kobe, Japan. It's American headquarters are in Orange County, just minutes from where Tiger Woods grew up.

Knight somehow managed to meet with the product development team at the company, including its founder, Kiachiro Onitsuka. When asked what his company name was, Knight, who had not thought the question through, uttered, "Blue Ribbon Sports."

What Knight had done was convince Onitsuka that he was the next great distributor for their product in America. Onitsuka first began manufacturing shoes when he discovered that melting wax at a Buddhist altar was a way to make the soft footbed for athletic shoes. His entrance into the market was making basketball shoes. Before long, Knight and Bill Bowerman, Knight's former track coach at the University of Oregon, were entrepreneurs.

Using a waffle iron and pliable rubber for the outsole, they began constructing the new Tiger footwear. Blue Ribbon Sports started in 1964 at the persistence of a 20-something former track rat at Oregon. The small business on paper now had real players. Knight was the point man for this garage-based business. This company eventually grew into what is now Nike.

Thirty-four years later, consider the infatuation Knight had for Tiger Woods in 1996. Just down the road from Beaverton in Cornelius, Oregon, a slender 21-year-old Stanford sophomore was lighting up the competition in the U.S. Amateur at Pumpkin Ridge. Knight roamed the gallery that week. He saw two Stanford teammates, Woods and Kribel, battle in the semifinals. Woods outlasted his teammate 3 and 1. In the finals, Woods was in familiar territory. The morning round left Woods staring at a 5-down deficit to Steve Scott, a University of Florida golfer, after the first 18 holes—the same margin by which he trailed Kuehne in 1994.

Woods cut the deficit to two when he won the 21st, 22nd and 23rd holes with birdie, birdie and par. Still 2-down standing on the 16th tee, Woods again went birdie, birdie, par to tie the match. On the second playoff hole (the par-3 10th) Woods two-putted from eight feet for the historic title. He completed a run that may never be equalled in amateur match-play competition. He won 18 consecutive matches. From 1994 to 1996, Tiger Woods played 18 of the best amateur players in the game and sent each one home for the summer.

The Pacific Northwest has always been kind to Woods. "I was 16 when I played at the Hogan Cup at Riverside Golf Club, and I played very well. I think our team won individually. The next was the U.S. Junior title (Waverley Country Club, Portland), and I won that. And then I won at Royal Oaks, which is just across the border," said Woods.

After the 1996 U.S. Amateur, Tiger was a hot commodity, just like the Tiger shoes in 1962. Knight had little to prove at this point in his amateur career, but how ironic. Just two kids who went to Stanford to study business—Knight learning how to create a shoe company from scratch and Woods, learning how to manage the millions he would receive for his knack for smacking a golf ball. The Tiger shoe was Knight's first step into Nike, and it all happened in the year of the Tiger. Onitsuka produced parts of their Tiger shoes from wax melted at a Buddhist altar. And now, Tiger Woods at the behest of his mother Kultida ventured annually to a Buddhist temple near Los Angeles. Tida Woods insists the pilgrimage is made with respect and to re-awaken them spiritually.

"The comparison to Nike's early years is just a fun coincidence," says president of Nike golf, Bob Wood. There is no pretending that Nike is the financial soul of Tiger Woods. With a contract estimated at close to $40 million, the shoes feel pretty comfortable on his feet. But what about Nike's overall commitment to Woods? "We are always looking at ways to improve our relationship. His (golf ball) deal is up in two years, and we will talk at that point," said Wood. He added, "The only golfer Phil Knight has ever been involved with is Tiger." Financially, Woods went from a zero-based amateur at Pumpkin Ridge in 1996 to the jack o' lantern of Nike Golf in the next millennium.

The years 1964-1971 are considered Nike's and Phil Knight's Tiger years. Back then, Knight was just a 20-something maverick with an idea. Knight's disputes with Tiger shoes actually ended in a lawsuit.

Now, Nike is locked in a lawsuit with Titleist over misleading television commercials. Woods is in the middle of a two-company tug-of-war.

Will history show that 1996 to 2010 are the Tiger years in golf? Knight certainly had his eye on the Tiger in 1994, but by the time he claimed his third U.S. Amateur title in Nike's backyard in 1996, the CEO of the sporting world was not about to let the Tiger out of the cage.

Never mind that Woods didn't finish his degree at Stanford. College golf for Woods was like the Canon Cup. Golf, the most individual sport on the planet, was made into a team event for someone else's benefit. "We had a pretty good run in college. As freshmen, we were called the best college golf team ever on paper. There was Notah Begay, Casey Martin, William Yanigasawa, Steve Burdick, and me," said Woods.

Woods had watched as a high school senior as Stanford edged Justin Leonard's Texas team in 1994 to win the national championship. Two years later he was leading the Stanford team at the Honors Course in Chattanooga, Tennessee. His first three rounds (69-67-69) set him apart from the field. His final-round 80 was enough for the NCAA individual title, but it wasn't good enough to count toward his team's total. His teammates roared that the NCAA champion couldn't even post a final round that made a difference. The crowds at the Honors Course, coupled with the lack of security, made the Stanford sophomore a trapped college golfer, playing one of America's most difficult layouts.

"I knew from the response to Tiger at that tournament that the young man was going to have to handle more than just his game," said coach Wally Goodwin. His NCAA title was also a fond farewell to college golf. If he could shoot 80 in the final round of the NCAAs and win, he might be ready for the next level, the PGA Tour."

Wally Goodwin spends August in "the middle of nowhere" Wyoming (actually about 120 miles from Casper in the northeast corner of the state) on a ranch that his family has owned since the 1800s. Five generations of Goodwins have developed the cattle ranch. Two days before Woods played in his first PGA Tour event as a professional, he called Goodwin and got the usual early riser out of bed. "Coach," Tiger said, "I'm going to turn pro in Milwaukee."

Goodwin was startled by Woods' voice in the early hours of the morning. He responded, "Go on, go ahead and earn some money kid, and good luck."

Their relationship had begun in 1988 when Goodwin was in his second year at Stanford. There he noticed a young boy from Cypress, California, in the *Sports Illustrated*'s "Faces in the Crowd" section. Goodwin's wife was honored in a similar fashion two weeks prior. Goodwin was well within the NCAA guidelines to correspond with a 7th grader, so he carefully cut out the picture of Woods with the caption and did the same with the issue featuring his wife. He sent the cut-and-paste art along with a note to Woods congratulating him on his recent junior accomplishments.

When Goodwin got a letter back from Woods, he was dumbfounded by the quality of penmanship by Woods (then just 13). "It was really staggering that he was so poised in his letter," said Goodwin. Shortly after he received the letter from Woods, Goodwin was confronted with a trivial concern from his academic All-American-laden golf team.

"Here are these academic All-Americans-like Brad Greer, Donnie Christiansen, and Mark Funseth arguing about a trivial matter," said Goodwin. He quickly diverted their interests by telling them of a 13-year-old black boy who had just written him a letter. "I made a copy of the letter and handed it out to each player. There was just cold silence," said Goodwin.

Stanford's early recruiting efforts paid off. Goodwin tracked Tiger through his junior triumphs, and about two weeks before the signing period, he got a surprise call from Tida Woods. "Coach," she said. "When are you coming down for a home visit?" Goodwin wondered if a home visit was necessary, considering all the contact he had already made with Woods. Not wanting to mess up closing the deal on the biggest college golf signing ever, Goodwin headed south to Orange County for dinner with Tida, Earl, and Tiger.

As Goodwin was being entertained at the Woods house for dinner, Tiger spent the time switching hats from other universities. Goodwin said, "He would wear the Arizona hat, then switch to the UNLV hat. I just told him he wasn't fooling me."

Stanford had an early indication Woods was going to play for the Cardinal. Several players were so sure that Woods was heading to Palo Alto that a few of them (Notah Begay and Casey Martin) redshirted their junior year so that they would get an opportunity to play with Woods. Stanford was the defending national champion, and now it had Tiger Woods entering the mix.

Goodwin remembers, "The anticipation and our team on paper was so exceptional. But we just didn't respond." Stanford was not able to build on its stack of talent, including Woods, in 1994-95. "We might have had too much talent," said Goodwin. He starts listing the team, which consisted of three All-Americans: "Steve Burdick, Brad Lanning, Jerry Chang, William Yanisagawa, Casey Martin, Notah Begay, and Tiger," said Goodwin.

Woods' freshman year was void of preferential treatment. Notah Begay hounded Woods incessantly for being the new kid on the Cardinal team. "The one aspect about Tiger's freshman year that I can't shake was that he was so punctual. If the van was leaving at 6:30 a.m., he was there at 6:15 with his McDonald's orange drink, ready to go," said Goodwin.

Playing on the Cardinal golf team also meant you were automatically a member of Stanford's intramural basketball team. Begay was an all-state basketball player in New Mexico looking for additional help, but it didn't come from Woods. "I've seen Woods run a quarter mile, and he was so impressive. His body never quivered around the track. He certainly didn't have the same gift on a basketball court. He was so uncoordinated. He had a hard time catching a basketball, let alone shooting it," said Goodwin.

The team found Tiger's weaknesses and exposed them like an open wound. Begay and Martin also made it a habit of tracking down Woods at the Friday night frat party of the week to check on what they called "the worst dancer in the history of Stanford University."

It wasn't dancing that Woods cultivated at Stanford. It was his knack for fitness and sending the golf ball down the middle of the fairway. His call to Goodwin's Wyoming ranch that he was turning pro was both a beginning and an end. Goodwin went back to bed after Woods called, but when he woke up in the morning, he reflected on the experience he had with Woods over the past five years and said to his wife Nancy, "If every family created a foundation and cultivated the way Earl and Tida Woods have done, the world would be a better place."

When Woods turned pro at the 1996 Greater Milwaukee Open, it was his coming-out party on the PGA Tour. The press had asked Woods at the U.S. Open at Oakland Hills and again at the British Open at Royal Lytham & St. Anne's if his amateur days were numbered. Is this the time? It was the time, and Woods responded by earning $790,594 in eight events at the end of 1996. He won twice (Walt Disney/Oldsmobile Classic and the Las Vegas Invitational), which put him in 25th place on the money list. Has also entered the world rankings (top 50) at No. 33.

His visits to Nike headquarters became part of his routine. And Bob Wood, 44, who has been with Nike since 1980, watched his company rise with the popularity of the sport. Before Woods, the Nike golf division was slow to take root. "It was like being a bastard child at the family reunion," said Wood. And like Knight's early years, the genesis of the golf division was footwear. They started by making athletically designed golf shoes, that now make up approximately 35 percent of the golf footwear category.

With a direction, Nike started head-hunting potential users on the PGA Tour. Since Peter Jacobsen went to the University of Oregon and knew Phil Knight, this was a logical first step. It helped that Jacobsen knew Curtis Strange. They also shared the same agent, Hughes Norton at IMG. The first three or four years they saturated themselves in shoes and targeted Strange and Jacobsen as the Nike icons for golf. Wood said, "We got the footwear business rolling and then came Tiger Woods.

"Signing Tiger was a catalyst in terms of Nike becoming more serious about the golf category. The first thing we did in American baseball and football was go out and establish relationships. We went from not being in the football business to having a relationship with Bear Bryant, Joe Paterno, Woody Hayes. Our products have to meet the needs of the most demanding people in their sports, not that Curtis (Strange) and Peter (Jacobsen) weren't demanding. It's just that Tiger Woods was someone who was a perfect fit for us."

Woods grew up in Orange County wearing the Nike products before he signed with the company. The fact that the athletes he admired, like Michael Jordan and Ken Griffey Jr. (now his neighbor in Isleworth), represented the company certainly didn't hurt Nike's multimillion-dollar pitch. "He came to understand quickly that the process of him working with us on product is a real thing. We can show you tapes of Tiger in our labs, swinging on force plates to enhance the design of our traction-control golf shoes. People on Wall Street think we make this stuff up," said Wood.

The north campus is just opening. It is made up of four buildings named for Mia Hamm, Pete Sampras, Ken Griffey and Jerry Rice. Wood said, "Tiger is worthy of his own building, but we don't have enough people in the golf division to have our own building." Golf at Nike is considered "a business unit." Woods used to attend Nike golf business meetings in jeans and a t-shirt. Now he shows up in Armani suits. "And he is a product geek, totally," said Wood. He added, "Look at the stuff Mark O'Meara is wearing at the British Open in 1998, about five layers, and Tiger had on two layers." O'Meara, however, was able to shed a few layers when he hoisted the claret jug.

About 15 Nike employees work with Woods on product development from wind-wear to shoes. "So many athletes, like NBA players, just say give me a size 12 shoe, they don't care. That's not Tiger," said Wood. To many at Nike, Woods relates to the individual approach to athletics that started with Oregon runner Steve Prefontaine, whose nickname was "Pre." Prefontaine remains a symbol that personifies the Nike mission. He was an athlete who embodied the spirit to compete. He, unfortunately, met an untimely death in an auto accident in May of 1975. It was later that same year that Earl and Kultida Woods had their first child in Cypress, California, Eldrick "Tiger" Woods.

A quarter of a century later, Woods is characterized in a similar way for his emotions during intense competition. "What attracted Phil to Tiger was his heart and his competitive fire. It reminds him of people like Michael Jordan, John McEnroe, and Pre." For many on the University of Oregon campus, "Steve Prefontaine was a real guy, a working-class guy, an iconoclast, a rebel," said Wood. Nike prides itself on the attitude behind the skill. That's why Nike recently went after young Spaniard Sergio Garcia. Garcia signed with Adidas for apparel and Titleist for equipment. Wood nods that El Niño has skill, but he says, "Sergio is a great player, but I wouldn't trade one Tiger Woods for 50 Sergio Garcias."

THE EYE ON THE TIGER

Press conferences at junior golf events? It is like holding a pep rally at a chess tournament. The free-swinging innocence of junior golfers and their playground is not supposed to be invaded by microphones and questions. In this case, questions from the top mediums of the Atlanta market: CNN, TNT, NBC, CBS. They all had affiliate camera crews and microphones hooked to a table so they could get the sound bites and footage of a group of junior golfers, including Tiger Woods.

Only the press conference was like a bloodletting. The press was bent on getting a self-admonition from Woods. How do they get Tiger to say that he's the player to beat? How do they get the young African American to quip that he's the best junior golfer who ever lived? Questions started coming fast and furious to a 15-year-old just trying to compete in another event, to be just another kid. This media event did not involve a golf club or ball.

A question finally landed, and the sponge-like media braced for the response. There was a panel of four junior players, but the attention on Woods was obvious: "Do you feel you're the player to beat this week?"

Woods weighed the strength of the question against his effort to respond. He knew the words he was about to spill would be the thesis for tomorrow's lead in papers in Atlanta.

He started with a simple preface: "I think there are a lot of fine junior players at this event. I will be tested just like they will be tested. But, I would like to think I'm one of the players to beat."

The sub-headline in the morning paper said it all, *"Woods says he's the player to beat."* Woods didn't say that, but the media did. Woods realized the magnification power of a medium other than his mind, ability, and his 14 clubs. Even as a junior player, he realized that success breeds expectations, and sometimes the media gravitates toward the dramatic. Just like he does on the golf course.

STILL LEARNING

Golf is a humbling game, and Tiger learned early that if he was going to improve his game, he needed to take what his father and early teachers, Rudy Duran and John Anselmo, taught him and continue to learn. After he became the youngest to win the U.S. Junior Championship at Bay Hill in 1991, he gained an admirer. A lot of PGA Tour players didn't have time to check out a kid, but not Mark O'Meara.

"I watched him play at Bay Hill when he was 15, and I was very impressed with what I saw. Two years later, he came through central Florida with his father, Earl, around Christmastime and we played again. He shot 71 and I shot 64. Our friendship just stuck," said O'Meara.

He capped off that summer with a return trip to the Canon Cup and his spot on the West team with captain Chris Haack. Woods joined mates like Trip Kuehne and Brian Bateman from earlier summer tournaments. They played at the Eisenhower Golf Course at the Air Force Academy in Colorado Springs, and the Canon Cup saw the West beat the East 29 1/2 - 20 1/2. What may be more important than the win was the maturation of the then 15-year-old Woods.

At the kickoff long-drive contest, the players were trying to distract the junior on the tee with comments like, "Noonan," and their verbal assault inflamed each player. That is, until the youngest player on either team stepped up to hit. Woods knew he had a chance to outdistance the competition. As he settled over the ball, he couldn't seem to get comfortable. The noise began to escalate. Woods stepped away from the ball. All of a sudden, the feverish pitch of chattering junior golfers was punctuated by a gavel-like look from Woods. The place went stone-cold silent. "I realized the respect he had then, and I couldn't believe the kids responded like that," said the AJGA's Pete Ripa.

Once again, he was the youngest competitor for either squad. Woods' intention was to learn from the older, more experienced kids, a lesson encouraged by his father. Woods went to his captain, Chris Haack, and asked if he could be paired with

Brian Bateman. Bateman was an AJGA lifer who had risen from one of the strongest young boys (13-14-year-olds) to a dominant player in the older boys' division. Bateman had just signed a letter of intent to join his good friend Harry Rudolph at Oklahoma State to play for coach Mike Holder. Bateman was a gregarious sort who, at the time, still called Tiger "Eldrick."

Haack paired Woods and Bateman for the best-ball competition. After both players hit their tee shots on the first hole of their match, Bateman and Woods began to talk about their pairing.

Woods said, "I asked to be your partner in the best ball."

Bateman, a native of Monroe, Louisiana, who had a thick bayou drawl, said, "Why did you pick me?"

Woods' response was matter of fact: "Because you're the best. The only way I am going to improve is by playing with the best."

Bateman just shook his head and headed to his tee shot.

After his win at the Deutsche Bank SAP Tournament in Germany and his triumphant win on the Nicklaus carpet at Muirfield Village, Woods was asked about the probability of not facing Seve (Ballesteros) and Nick (Faldo) at Brookline for the Ryder Cup. He simply said, "To not have two players like that on their team will be different. Because I always want to play against the best. To have that challenge, it feels pretty good when you do win," said Woods.

Bateman reflects now, "I realized he was driven to succeed, but back then he was just a skinny kid; he was only 15." He added, "He really didn't hit the ball that far back then." Woods has always responded to the competition, "I always like to challenge myself. That was one way to improve. Like the way Magic

Johnson played against Larry Bird. I realized how to get better. And I practiced quite a bit as a kid," said Woods.

He practiced so much as a three-year-old that he shot 48 for nine holes. "I grew up really watching my dad hit golf balls in the garage," said Woods. His father, Earl, would evaluate a course and arbitrarily make up a number that would be considered a good score for his son. And that number would be par for the hole.

As Woods checks into the next millennium at age 24, he has a lot of miles on his golf game. He has used his father, Bateman and other junior players as role models for his own game. He heard the heckling by kids at the Air Force Academy, and now he is hearing the same verbal assaults on the PGA Tour. He is measuring his game and accomplishments against the elite. Now he's the role model.

By the time he turned professional in 1996, he had already played in 14 PGA Tour events and six majors. Not a bad transition from the junior and amateur levels. The only one in the golf world who was not easily impressed by Woods' rise was the late Gene Sarazen. Sarazen, when asked about the youthfulness of Woods in relation to his accomplishments, said, "What's the big deal? I had two majors by the time I was 20." In 1922, Sarazen did win the PGA and the U.S. Open. Woods won the PGA at the spry age of 23 with Sergio on his heels. The U.S. Open continues to be on his short list.

At the U.S. Open in 1999, Duval was being asked about the finger he burned while boiling water for instant coffee. Phil Mickelson was answering questions about the birth of his first child, and Woods was left to answer questions about racist remarks his father had made about people in Scotland in *Icon* magazine. Defending his dad, he said, "My dad is not like that. My dad knows Scotland is a wonderful place."

Earl Woods would roam the course with Tiger during his junior days, listening to jazz, the likes of Ella Fitzgerald on headphones. He would be so taken by the free-flowing music that he would whistle out loud. It was the same jazz music that Tiger's parents exposed their son to when he was five days old.

Tiger's not whistling about the verbal jazz his father has created since he arrived on the PGA Tour. From his disdain for not being included in the Ryder Cup at Valderrama to his remarks on Scotland, Woods had to squelch media sentiment. Woods also admits that his dad is his cornerstone for counsel. "He's always been there, not only as a father figure, but as a mentor, a best friend, and a counselor. If there is anyone in this world I can turn to at any given time, it would be him," Woods said.

Does the golfing world have enough patience for Tiger Woods? He won his first green jacket in 1997 and resurfaced in 1999 with a retooled swing, only to regain his top world ranking. He let his longtime agent Hughes Norton go and hooked on with Mark Steinberg. As he spins out of his one-year swing-funk, could his time be now?

Mark O'Meara said, "Let's give Tiger three or four years and see what happens." Tigermania hit hard in 1997. The runaway Masters created expectations that maybe only a surging player named Sergio Garcia can squelch. As for Woods, his explosive emergence in 1997 created expectations, but he realized the summer of 1998 was a cooling-off period. Woods compares it to women's tennis: "You can look at it in today's time with Martina Hingis, when she burst on the scene in '97. She won quite a few tournaments, and all the fans wanted to see her. Now she's been around a few years, she wins four or five tournaments a year. The eagerness factor to go out and look and watch has diminished." David Duval and the intrigue of Sergio Garcia have allowed Woods to share the stage, but his late-season run in 1999 is rekindling the Nicklaus-type comparisons.

THE SUMMER OF 1997

In 1997, "Tigermania" had hit full tilt. As Tiger puts it, "They're getting used to me." Woods won the Mercedes Championship in January, a tournament in Bangkok, Thailand, in February, and then came to Augusta with an attitude. He played the front nine at the Masters in 40. He then pounced on Augusta like it was a ragdoll, bringing home a 30 on the back nine for a one-day total of 70. Tiger was playing a different game at the Masters. He averaged over 320 yards off the tee boxes all week. He did not have one three-putt on the slippery Augusta greens, and Amen Corner was just another track.

Tiger Woods took a month off after Augusta, as Hughes Norton of IMG fielded endorsement offers like Brooks Robinson. He became the first player on a golf course to break the $2-million mark in a single season, and he had just turned 21. It was a maddening pace ushered in by his Masters win.

Little kids began taking to driving ranges, moms called the local recreation departments to enter their kids in tournaments, and the Golf Foundation, trying to keep up with the skyrocketing popularity of the game. The National Golf Foundation keeps the kind of statistics that one should read for insomnia. In 1997, it released a report that said the number of beginners jumped 52 percent. In January of 1997, when Woods aced the 10th hole at the Phoenix Open, the roar was deafening. He raised the roof on the complacent game. He was beginning to take on the persona of a 5-iron-hitting rock star. At the Byron Nelson Classic, Woods said, "It (Tigermania) reached the highest level."

Soon after the Byron Nelson, Woods started grading his game after tournaments, and some PGA Tour veterans like Brad Faxon and Davis Love III bristled at the suggestion that the kid had room for improvement. Never mind that after he won the Western Open in 1997, the rest of the year was a disappointment. He did not finish better than tied for 19th in the next three majors. He lost to Constantino Rocca at the Ryder Cup, the same Rocca who had accompanied him in his record-setting final round at Augusta and beat him in Spain. The can't-miss kid suddenly became human.

Mark O'Meara counseled his friend. He played more practice rounds with Woods and surveyed Tiger's situation up close. "The game has changed. It is not the same as it was 12 years ago," said O'Meara. He remembers the days when there were a dozen people watching him play a practice round. He added, "Now there are thousands." O'Meara admits that the conduct of the fans may need to be harnessed. The decorum of the game has changed outside the gallery ropes. Woods agrees, especially when it comes to for late afternoon tee times. He laughingly admitted, "I remember in 1997, in the late afternoon, they got to be more vocal."

But Woods thinks that as his game has matured, so has the craziness experienced in 1997 with Tigermania. "I think that was the crescendo of the whole thing. I don't think it will ever get to that point again. I was new on the scene. I was there for the first time and won a major championship," Woods shrugged his shoulders.

Tiger admits that his swing has taken on a different plan and plane. In 1997, Woods was a pedal-to-the-metal player with booming tee shots and aggressive iron play. His swing, at the behest of his teacher Butch Harmon, has taken on a "more rounded" plane, which gives him more control. "If you look at videotapes you'll notice my swing plane is more rounded at the top. It's about the same length, but my left and right arm position are completely different. Hence, the golf club gets in front of me a little better, and I can use the true loft of the golf club," he said.

Woods reminded everyone during the changes the importance of being "patient." Harmon has shown Woods how he can shorten his backswing without reducing the expanse of his arc, but, changing the swing plane is a complex strategy. Just look at Jim Furyk's swing plane and then suggest that if he were to draw the club back like, say, Steve Elkington, he might have more success. Like the Nike insiders say, Woods is a geek when it comes to product, and he is a geek when it comes to the proper way to hit a golf ball. Getting the club head in the right position is, for the time being, more important than the speed with which the club head is traveling. Butch Harmon, following the 1998 British Open, approached Woods about rerouting his swing. Both Harmon and Woods knew the process would involve a gradual and delicate balance. But, as Harmon stated, "It was in the interest of making him a better player. And he understood the importance, and it was because he has matured as a player and person that he was able to handle it." The ability to replicate the swing and not revert back is now sometimes the poison.

Woods' short game has become the poison for other players. As evidenced by his summer of 1999 wins at the Memorial, the Western, and the PGA, Woods used a short game to dispel myths that his game was ruled from the tee boxes. He said, "Growing up as a kid, I used to throw golf balls in the trees and try to make pars and birdies. I love the challenge." Woods hit shots around the greens at both tournaments that were astounding. The prospect of Woods gaining a finesse short game to go with his power is a combination that will reverberate throughout the PGA Tour in the new millennium.

Woods also knows something about goal setting and creating a game that dominates week after week. Even as a junior, he set his lofty personal expectations. The generation before him had goals, but not Nicklaus-like goals. Johnny Miller, who emerged with ambition in the 1970s, said, "I never really had goals like Tiger." Miller knows that Woods is caught in a position of being an ambassador of the game, but his era has a few more distractions than those prevalent in the mid-'70s.

"I think Tiger has these goals and ambitions that will push him past a lot of the pain-in-the-butt stuff with the media and fans he has to deal with. I'm one of them too," he added.

As Mark O'Meara pointed out, "The game goes in cycles. If you look back from the beginning of time, guys get hot for a while. I know Tiger hasn't won the amount of tournaments that we all anticipated he will win. But I think it's just a matter of time."

As he rocketed through junior golf, amateur golf, and now the PGA Tour, Woods began to understand the importance of the word *patience*. Duval has shown a patience that matches his personality. For Woods, the adjustment is a little more difficult. O'Meara thinks patience might be the only aspect of Woods' game that would keep him from the next level. He went from junior golf to amateur golf as a young teenager. He went from college golf to the PGA Tour at the age of 20. Now he has burst onto the PGA Tour with electrifying abilities to hit the ball long. His first major gave rise to terminology like "Tigeresque" and "Tigermania."

It has always been about levels for Tiger Woods. He has always gone after the next plateau before he comes up for air. At the age of 16, he won the U.S. Junior and competed with the big boys at the U.S. Amateur. He competed in professional events while attending Stanford. Can his early perseverance push him to extraordinary numbers like Nicklaus, or will it burn out before he reaches the summit?

At the U.S. Open, he was reflecting on his meteoric rise through the game. "I was a junior golfer and nobody knew me. They maybe knew of me, but not to the extent that it is now. A lot has changed since then (junior golf), but one thing that has remained the same is that I love to play," said Woods.

The affirmations that his parents provided may carry Woods farther than anything in professional golf. His glass-half-full approach can create extraordinary results. Check out how many athletes have turned to sports psychologists for help on a positive approach to difficult situations. In his book *Thinking Body, Dancing Mind,* sports psychologist Jerry Lynch explores the notion. He visited the Penn State cross-country team, where, in a clinic, he offered a suggestion that the team "loves hills." The team adopted the approach and began overtaking teams on the most difficult part of the cross-country course. Woods has a similar approach, except he overtakes players on the hills of the world's toughest courses with gargantuan drives and an adept short game.

Positive frames of reference and visualization are the aspects of Woods' attitude that no one person can touch. This intangible factor alone is perhaps his greatest asset. Arm strength, trunk rotation, and overall club-head speed help, but consider the fact that golf is a game marked by an unquestionable small margin of error. Put Woods in that element with the skill, an unquenchable thirst for excelling with positive thoughts, and the results are staggering. Once Woods gets into position for a championship, he rarely fails to convert. The 1999 World Golf Championship-NEC, the PGA, the Western Open, the Memorial, the 1998 BellSouth. In 1997, at the Disney/Oldsmobile Classic. His approach to the sport nets him results and explains why players like Brad Faxon call his ability "unparalleled." Leonard is Kite-like,

AJGA

Phil Mickelson on the 10th hole of Horseshoe Bend Country Club in 1987.

Mickelson's short game was proficient long before he arrived at Arizona State.

Arizona State Sports Information

MASTERS OF THE MILLENNIUM

Tiger Woods at age seventeen teeing off at the Taylor Made Woodlands Classic in 1993.

AJGA

Tiger Woods as a freshman golfer for Wally Goodwin at Stanford.

Stanford Sports Information

MASTERS OF

Justin Leonard with his Texas-Oklahoma Junior Championship trophy.

Byron Nelson with a proud champion of the AJGA junior event at Las Colinas.

THE MILLENNIUM

Justin Leonard
with a persimmon
driver in 1992 at
the University of
Texas.

Greenside play
and the ability to
convert has always
been a Justin
Leonard trademark.

MASTERS OF

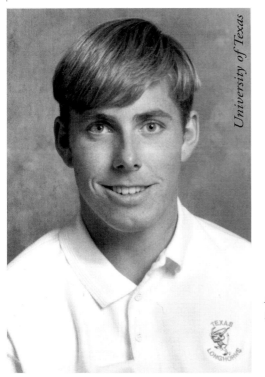

University of Texas

Leonard was a four-time
All-Southwest Conference
selection.

Stewart Cink and
the white bucket-
hatted Leonard shake
hands after Cink
defeated Leonard in
a semi-final match at
the 1989 American
Junior Classic.

AJGA

THE MILLENNIUM

Cliff Fischer

Ford Fischer points to his first tournament found in the '70s.

Cliff Fischer

Ford Fischer may not be a twenty-something player on the PGA Tour, but he's one of Randy Smith's bright young junior players.

A floppy golf hat and confidence. Duval had both playing national junior golf.

AJGA

Duval was a four-time All-American at Georgia Tech.

Georgia Tech Sports Information

The talented David Duval was a free spirit at Georgia Tech, which his teammates and coach Puggy Blackmon dealt with in different ways.

Georgia Tech Sports Information

Before IMG and Titleist entered the picture, Duval grooved a game with long hair and an attitude.

Georgia Tech Sports Information

MASTERS
OF THE
MILLENNIUM

Mickelson is Seve-like, Duval is Nicklaus-like and Woods is like no other player in the world.

Sitting in a board room on the Nike campus, Bob Wood recently started to explain the state of the golf industry over the last two years in a golf division business meeting. Despite the exorbitant television contract negotiated in 1997, despite the rise in the popularity in the game, he said, "The last two years have not been banner years for a lot of people in the golf business."

Wood had planned to initiate a 20-minute state-of-the-industry address. The presentation lasted for an hour and ten minutes because a 23-year-old PGA Tour player wanted to ask so many questions. "They were really good questions on what was going on with the other side of the game," said Wood. There is no reason the young man driving the sports bus needs to know about the transmission, but Woods wants to continue to understand how the sport operates off the fairways.

As a junior golfer growing up in California, he would show up at the Heartwell par 3 in Long Beach. Heartwell is a little jewel of a par 3 that now hosts hundreds of junior golfers that are Woods wannabes. The light stanchions allowed him to traverse the layout even at dark. And now Woods has gone from the same lights at Heartwell to the champion of the Showdown at Sherwood. Woods was quickly down two holes to Duval at Sherwood, exactly where Woods likes to make his move. By the 12th hole, he was 3 up. As they teed off on 17, Woods just needing a halve for the win, and the lights that were installed for the prime-time event, illuminating two of the masters of the millennium. After the round, Woods said, "I grew up playing under lights like this, so I'm used to this."

A Different Rivalry?

"Fun" was what Sergio Garcia called the 1999 PGA Championship. He said, "It was the best week of my life." At 19 years of age, the young Spanish sensation pushed Woods to the limit at Medinah. The last major of the century, and the field was reduced to the two youngest players—Tiger versus El Niño. Two different countries representing the same kind of game—the way the game will continue to be played. Woods calls it "an aggressive game, creative around the greens with a great deal of emotion."

Woods was not accustomed to being challenged. After all, he was looking at a replica of himself, four years earlier. Woods said, "His body language exudes confidence. He plays with a lot of emotion and has a tremendous amount of fight in him. Woods tapped in for par on the 72nd hole for a one-stroke win over Garcia. He gave the Spaniard a hug and said, "Great playing."

The boisterous Chicago crowd got behind Sergio's power surge on Sunday. They chanted "Sergio!" Sergio!" Woods enjoyed a cinco-stroke lead until Garcia's birdie went sinko on 13. Woods took aim on the 13th tee and hit a 6-iron over the green, then followed through with two bold chips. Two putts later, and the bullfight was on. Woods' bogey on 16 left the door slightly ajar for the fearless wonder from Spain. Could this be the rivalry the media were trying to create?

In a city once ruled by Michael Jordan, did Tiger Woods become the three-peat kid on the PGA Tour? He won the 1997 Western Open going away in 1997 and 1999. The trilogy in Chicago earned Woods his second major and his 11th win on Tour. Comparisons to Nicklaus started to fly. Nicklaus had three majors and 12 wins by the same point in his career. But as Woods pointed out, "Nicklaus had won the grand slam by the age of 26. I'd like to do the same." He has two years to punctuate the mark, and as he put it, "I just need to keep giving myself the chances. A lot of different things can happen if you just get yourself into position."

Walking down the 12th fairway, Woods' caddie, Steve Williams, turned to Tiger and said, "Golf is a little different than it was 20 years ago." Williams was referring to the raucous crowd that thought it was at a Black hawks game instead of a major golf championship. The game is changing inside the gallery ropes and outside the gallery ropes.

The last major of the century was a blank canvas that slowly took on a generational tug of war as the week progressed. There was 54-year-old Hale Irwin, in contention after 36 holes. And a group of 40-somethings, Jay Haas, Lanny Wadkins, and Nick Price, all showed that age really doesn't matter—until Sunday. Nick Price went out in 32, but stumbled on the back nine, leaving center stage to the brash young twosome. Stewart Cink, 26, part of the collective 20-somethings near the lead at Medinah, hung around on Sunday to finish fourth.

To Woods, the rivalry does not exist. He insisted, "I don't think there is a rivalry. There are too many good players in their 20s: Justin Leonard, Phil Mickelson, David Duval, Ernie Els. Guys like Lee Westwood and Darren Clarke are exceptional players. There will be a handful of players who lead us into the next millennium," said Woods.

When he arrived in Orlando to play his first-ever Canon Cup, Woods did not realize he would call Isleworth down the street his home, as a young professional. Then again, Woods is on a course that some brashly predicted, but no one person could have expected. As we bridge the millennia, what more can he do to revolutionize the game of golf?

THE MICKELSONIAN WAY

The clouds looked like giant tumbleweeds. They began to roll in like the heat so often does in Edmond, Oklahoma. On the practice range, college players covered their golf bags, blossomed their umbrellas and headed for the clubhouse at Oak Tree Golf Club, the site of the 1989 NCAA Championship. At first, the rain began to fall softly. One by one, the players marched for cover. Just then, with a determined look in his eyes, Phil Mickelson took the cover off his driver to begin an imaginary 18 holes on the Oak Tree range. A stately club, Oak Tree has long been recognized by its tree logo, which depicts a grandiose oak tree with perfect symmetry.

As Mickelson pegged his first range ball, the rain's pace quickened, and the deluge engulfed every stitch of greenery. Mickelson donned a rainsuit and just went through a patient pace—no forced movements—preparing for each shot of his mindful round. The rain soon began to pelt the Arizona State freshman with a force that required him to adjust his stance regularly. About 30 minutes of persistent rain showers pounded the focused golfer. Players inside the clubhouse just shook their heads in disbelief as Mickelson hit calculated shot after calculated shot. The players and coaches in the pro shop joked in Caddyshack fashion, "Your honor, if I were you, I'd keep playing. I don't think the really heavy stuff's coming down for quite a while." Casual water collected on the range, and the focused Sun Devil freshman was just beginning his back nine when an onlooker heading for cover asked, "Phil, what the hell are you doing?"

Mickelson flipped his club and rotated his head as if to say, "I just made the turn, and I'm 3 under." His study of the duty at hand was purely Micklesonian, and while he was the last player to leave the practice tee that day, he was the first player on top of the leader board at the end of the Tournament. As a freshman, he captured the NCAA individual title with a 7-under-par 281, five days shy of his 19th birthday.

Previous freshman NCAA champs have included Curtis Strange (Wake Forest, 1974) and Billy Ray Brown (Houston, 1982). The first freshman ever to win the NCAA Championship was Ben Crenshaw in 1971, when he led his Texas team to the National Championship. Crenshaw gave an indication that he was going to be a successful college player by playing in his first PGA Tour event in the summer of 1970. About a month before the U.S. Open, he qualified to play in his first major, at Hazeltine National Golf Course in Chaska, Minnesota.

In 1970, around this same time of the year, Philip Anthony Mickelson and his wife, Mary, were searching for the perfect home in the San Diego, California, area for their growing family. Mary was eight months' pregnant with their second child. Their first child, Tina, who was just a toddler, would soon have a little brother or sister. Traveling around, looking at homes on a warm May afternoon in 1970 was not a lot of fun for Mary Mickelson. Their journey seemed unending, but one afternoon it took them to a new development in San Diego and a modest house on Wenrich Road. That's when Phil saw something he liked. "I realized they had made an engineering error. It was a pie-shaped lot probably three times larger than most," said Phil. He added, "And they brought in all this extra soil. "I told Mary that the lot itself had a lot of value." Sold. Phil and Mary quickly settled into their home with the expansive backyard.

Phil, a commercial pilot, had little time for the happenings in the world of golf. With their second child due any day, the Mickelsons had little reason to follow what was happening in the Midwest, in Minnesota of all places. Billy Casper, Gene Littler, Dave Hill, Gary Player, and Bert Yancey had their sights on the second major of the year, as they tuned up at Hazeltine Golf Course, designed by Robert Trent Jones. The former cropland had been converted into a course with an unconventional layout that was completed in 1962. Now, eight years later, the best golfers were descending on the transformed farmland to show their skills against a design many of the PGA Tour called unfair.

"It is a good farm ruined," said Dave Hill before the Tournament. On Tuesday, June 16, the field traversed the Jones layout in practice rounds and came away with differing opinions of the course. Players like Littler, Casper, Hill, and little-known amateur Ben Crenshaw each envisioned his own prospects for the week at Hazeltine. The warm June temperatures were not as severe as the windy conditions. Once the championship started, meteorologists registered wind gusts up to 40 mph. Everyone agreed that the U.S. Open would produce a formidable champion. And everyone agreed, even the USGA, that the U.S. Open would someday return to Hazeltine.

On the Tuesday before the 1970 U.S. Open at Hazeltine, in a world far removed from the decorum of a major championship, Phil and Mary Mickelson, witnessed a miracle, the birth of their second child, a boy. They named him Philip Alfred Mickelson . Fatherhood was an institution that Phil Mickelson Sr. had not only a reverence for, but a passion for. Passing on his name was something Phil Sr. had often thought of during his wife's pregnancy, but he did not really appreciate the significance of the moment until Philip was born.

A couple days after the birth, Phil Sr. and Mary Mickelson prepared birth announcements: the announcement declared that "the Mickelson *foursome* was now complete." A photo of Philip sitting on the nose of an airplane was a takeoff on the mythic stork delivery. Like most young couples, the Mickelsons juggled nurturing their daughter, Tina, their newborn son, Philip, home maintenance, and careers. They had little time for the sports page, but had they looked at the accounts of the week, they would have noticed that a player named Tony Jacklin had captured the U.S. Open at Hazeltine. Jacklin was the first-ever Englishman to win the U.S. Open. A sub-plot to the week's story was that of a youngster named Crenshaw making the cut and finishing tied for 36th.

Back in San Diego, neighbors were coming over and introducing themselves to the Mickelsons and checking on their new baby boy. There was even a 17-year-old kid down the street named Craig Stadler who was busy in junior golf. He would win the World Junior Championship that summer. Stadler would end up at the University of Southern California and later claim the 1973 U.S. Amateur.

The Mickelsons were just trying to make ends meet and care for Tina and Philip. Mary Mickelson would send her toddler son into the backyard so she could cook. "I would look out the kitchen window and see Philip just watching his dad swing. And for the longest time, Philip would just stand there, holding golf balls in his hands and watching," she said. Phil's dad would swing his club in the backyard, and he said, "At that age, you want them to watch in front of you. Phil (Jr.) was always in front of me as I hit balls, mostly for safety."

A cut-down right-handed 3-wood soon found the tiny hands of the blond toddler, and so Philip began as a toddler where most junior players begin—in the backyard. Dad would show the right-handed pendulum swing to Philip. "He would always stand in front of me, mirroring my movements," said Phil Sr. "He would stand facing me and draw the club back, *like a left-hander,* and hit it with the back of the club. He hit the ball awfully good."

Not wanting to interfere with his son making solid contact with the ball, Phil Sr. rounded off the face of the 3-wood so that it became a very narrow-headed instrument. "He just wore that club out. We would stand in the backyard and hit ball after ball," said Phil Sr. The cut-down junior wood, Phil's first club, is now encased in a shadow box in Phil and Amy Mickelson's Scottsdale, Arizona, home. The club is complete with electrical tape, the shaft is nicked and the face is worn thin by hundreds of practice shots. What started as mirror imitation of his dad's golf swing slowly evolved into a smooth left-handed stroke for young Philip.

"TO ME EVERY HOUR OF THE LIGHT AND DARK IS A MIRACLE. EVERY CUBIC INCH OF SPACE IS A MIRACLE."
—WALT WHITMAN

For the first 10 years of Philip's junior days, the Mickelson backyard featured a shortly mowed area that contained a cup and a tee box that father and son gradually wore down to the soil. It was an unassuming practice area, but the setting was enough to endear the game to Philip.

At the age of six, Philip entered his first junior golf Tournament. Mickelson's early years in San Diego County gave little indication that he was destined for greatness. From 1976 to 1979, the young Philip Mickelson (ages 6-9) did not win any events. He played in 53 Tournaments and did not bring home one first-place trophy. The left-hander also met another six-year-old boy named Harry Rudolph, from nearby La Jolla, who had the same enthusiasm for the game.

At that time, the San Diego Junior Golf Association (San Diego JGA), founded by John Brown in 1952, was coming of age. With graduating classes in the 1970s that included future PGA Tour players Craig Stadler, Jack Renner, Lon Hinkle, Lennie Clements, Scott Simpson, and Mark Weibe, the San Diego JGA was being recognized as one of the strongest youth golf programs nationwide.

In 1980, Phil Sr. medically retired from the airlines and he spent a great amount of time redesigning the backyard. He wanted more of a true golfing environment for his children, Tina, Philip, and Tim, just a toddler. It was a two-year project that slowly became more and more complex. Phil Sr. studied books that detailed the makeup of the subsoil. He talked with local experts on the installation of the greens' drain tile. He wanted the mixture of gravel to sand to be just right so that the burgeoning practice area, with proper watering and mowing, would be just like a "full-fledged green."

As a 10-year-old trying to improve, Philip would help his dad tend the backyard. As time passed, the Mickelsons' backyard evolved into a green, sand trap, collar, and chipping area. The sand trap was banked on one side with a deep face and short lip on the other side, so that a player could pitch or roll the ball out. The slightly raised (six inches) green has a gradual slope. It is well defined with a tightly groomed collar and throat for aptly played approach shots to enter the green.

The once-humble Mickleson backyard had been slowly transformed into a unique practice setting. It went from a modest, municipal-like environment to a fully contoured and manicured strand of nature—from the stark beginnings to the west coast version of the Augusta par 3. "We would have neighbors and friends over and they would say, 'What golf course is in the area? I don't remember one?" said Phil Sr. with a greenskeeper's pride.

The Bermuda grass backyard soon became a proving ground for the entire Mickelson family. The grass would go dormant in the fall. It was nature's way of saying take a recess from golf. Yet, Philip would continue to practice.

As the backyard began to take shape, so did Philip's game. As a 10-year-old, he won the Optimist Junior World Championship, amid a field of just fewer than 100 juniors on the tricky par-54 Presidio Hills Golf Course. Longtime PGA Tour player Morris Hatalsky was once asked how he mastered the greens at Pinehurst No. 2, and his answer was a simple, "These greens are nothing compared to Presidio Hills." Mickelson continued his summer by winning four of the 15 San Diego JGA events he entered and finishing runner up in seven others. He was beginning to gain confidence, and he was captivated by the game.

"EVERY CHILD IS AN ARTIST. THE PROBLEM IS HOW TO REMAIN AN ARTIST ONCE HE GROWS UP."
—PABLO PICASSO

Philip learned about the creative complexities of the short game in his backyard. The triangular Mickelson practice area accepts a shot between 44 and 60 yards. To this day, it's still maintained with lights and is still the stage for family—reunion grudge matches. A formidable pairing is the PGA Tour left-hander chipping off against his right-handed brother Tim, a junior golfer at Oregon State for coach Mike Ketcham. Phil Mickelson earned a reputation for his short game throughout junior and amateur golf.

"I attribute a lot of my short-game success because I would hit so many shots. Sometimes I'd get bored hitting the same shots over and over in my backyard," said Mickelson. He would explain at junior Tournaments, "I have a chipping and putting green in my backyard, and I practice so many shots." Kids would give Phil quizzical looks as if to say, "Sure, Phil, whatever." But as junior days wore on, so did the artistry of the left-handed-playing junior from San Diego, especially his short game. Mickelson was the wizard of Weinrich Road, and he was beginning to take his show on the road.

As a child with an imagination, Mickelson looked to professional golf for a role model. A Spaniard named Seve Ballesteros had a charisma and a short game that quickly caught the attention of Mickelson. Ballesteros attacked a golf course with fiery emotion, and at age 22 he won his first major title (the 1979 British Open) at Royal Lytham & St. Anne's. In that Tournament, Ballesteros hit a wild shot into a car parking lot on the 70th hole. He somehow managed to get the ball on the green, making a birdie. He edged Jack Nicklaus and Ben Crenshaw by three strokes for the claret jug.

Impressionable, Mickelson aspired to do incredible "Ballesteros-like things" in his backyard, and then follow up by executing his shots in competition at Presidio Hills and Balboa Park.

"Ball placement was important in his swing, and eventually, he would play games to see what trajectory of shot the green would accept," said his father. "Phil spent so many hours in the backyard. He would play it off the fruit trees, and he knew exactly what places on the green accepted a well-played shot." Mickelson invented ways to strike the ball that made it look simple. He was adept at putting English on the golf ball. From the fairway, he could send a low cut-shot into a green and spin the ball, drawing it in different directions. The precision of the shot showed the maturity of his game. After all, he was just having fun in the backyard.

Mickelson went on to win 34 of the next 109 local (San Diego JGA) Tournaments he entered and was named the San Diego JGA Player of the Year in 1985, 1986 and 1987. On the national scene, Mickelson won two events as a 14-year-old (the Lake Tahoe Memorial Junior and the Mission Hills Desert Junior). At his first AJGA event at Edgewood Tahoe, Chris Haack was so captivated by the 14-year-old that he asked the staff to check out his game on the range. "He was hitting balls from the range like I had never seen before," remembers Haack.

At the time, Haack, AJGA director of communication, Scott Hodoval, Jeff Monday and Steve Hamblin left the Tournament headquarters to examine the junior golfer from San Diego. "His swing and confidence hitting balls were so evident," said Haack. Monday, who is now the director of operations for the PGA Senior Tour, remembers hearing Haack incessantly boasting about the "kid from Sandyago." Haack would tell Monday, Hamblin and Hodoval, "This kid is going to win in bunches."

Mickelson did win in bunches. He claimed the Rolex Tournament of Champions from 1986 to 1988 and was the National AJGA Player of the Year each of those years. Twelve AJGA championships—four more than Tiger Woods—came home to Weinrich Road. Even though Mickelson's numbers are impressive, he left an impression both on and off the junior golf circuit that will take more than the progression of Justin Leonard, David Duval, Tiger Woods, Charles Howell, David Gossett, Ryan Hybl, and Hunter Mahan to erase.

"FAME USUALLY COMES TO THOSE WHO ARE THINKING ABOUT SOMETHING ELSE."
—OLIVER WENDELL HOLMES, JR.

As a junior, what also separated Mickelson on the course from the rest of the bag-toting pack went well beyond his silky southpaw swing. It exceeded his calm temperament and demeanor. Mickleson's matter-of-fact innocence was so innocent and unusual that he made even his most hated enemies shake their heads in admiration. In 1987, at the age of 17, Mickelson could have elected to putt his ball on the last hole of the Rolex Tournament of Champions. Instead, he chose a wedge to play on his fourth shot on the par-5 18th. Mickelson strolled to take out the pin and returned to his ball. After taking a few practice swings, he flipped his club in Mickelsonian style and addressed the ball. He calmly stroked the ball with an artful precision. The ball rolled square in the center of the cup to seal the AJGA Tournament of Champions, his second consecutive major junior championship.

It wasn't his chipping that attracted a throng of listeners at the trophy presentation. Mickelson's dry humor and wit attracted more than a typical small gathering to the post-Tournament festivities. "I think he had a habit of saying the wrong thing at the right time," said Harry Rudolph, one of Mickelson's longtime junior rivals. The audience would often grow larger due to the element of the unexpected. The speech would often develop like a mosaic of thoughts: *I want to thank the greens superintendent for having the course in great shape. I want to thank my mom for getting a second job and allowing me the opportunity to play in more Tournaments. I want to thank Mr. Gray for giving me a ride to the course all week. Thanks to the Tournament staff, everything went very smooth, tee times... Mr. Batten for the beautiful scoreboard. Oh, and I want to thank the waitress at Confetti's for giving me an extra scoop of mint chocolate chip. Thanks to Horseshoe Bend for the nice range balls. To Mr. Rick Bannerot at Rolex, thanks for sponsoring a great event. Chris Haack, thanks for the advice.*

Mickelson speeches were purely Mickelsonian. They were innocently rehearsed and genuinely polite. "What Phil liked to do was unbelievable. He would thank anyone and everyone associated with the Tournament. From the head pro to the shuttle driver from the airport, that was just Phil," said Steve Hamblin, the AJGA's executive director. One prevailing theme ran throughout his acceptance speeches. He always thanked his mom for getting a second job. His mom, Mary, worked at a retirement center in the San Diego area so Philip could afford to play in national junior events. She was recently recognized as the March of Dimes Mother of the Year (1998) for her contributions.

Mickelson's humility was on display later that year at the American Junior Classic at Innisbrook in November. In a semifinal match, he was paired with Nicky Goetze. Goetze was a methodical junior player who epitomized stoicism. His sister Vicki was the young female version of Mickelson. She dominated play at the junior level from 1986 to 1990 With Mickelson and Goetze locked in a decidedly close duel, Mickelson's attention was momentarily diverted from the match. As he left a tee box on the back nine, he spotted a squirrel that decided to leave the security of the woods and check out the human activity. Mickelson was so captivated by the animal that he decided he was going to play dodge and weave with the furry rodent. With his bag on his shoulder, Mickelson darted left and right, trying to corner the squirrel for several minutes. His careless journey led him to the edge of the woods. Goetze and the small gallery continued to their tee shots. Jeff Monday, the referee for the match, could not believe his eyes.

"Here was Mickelson chasing a fox-squirrel like he was in his backyard, and he's in the semifinals of the biggest junior Tournament we have," said Monday. Once Mickelson exhausted his hunt, he just smiled his boyish grin and slothed to his tee shot.

In his final summer of junior golf (1988), Mickelson was approaching his last hole in AJGA competition. With a one-shot lead, he needed to guard against playing a long bunker shot to a pin guarded by water surrounding the green. "He knocked the shot three inches from the cup; at that time, I thought this kid is either stupid or fearless," said Haack. When Mickelson would accomplish an awe-inspiring shot, both as a junior and now on Tour, there was the grin. Part of Mickelson's junior show included the Jim Colbert-style flipped-up collar. Junior playing mate Trip Kuehne said, "That was just a little California cool. And the smile was just his way of saying I believe in myself."

Boyhood rival Harry Rudolph still sees the kid in Phil when he makes a shot in major competition. "There are definitely two sides to Phil Mickelson, and that smirk he has on his face when he holes a putt is definitely one side," said Rudolph.

Mickelson related everything he encountered to the game of golf. At one point, growing up, his obsession with the game went to extremes. He took a music appreciation course at University of San Diego High School. He was given an assignment that allowed the students to compare great composers to aspects of daily living. His mother remembers her creative son pioneered the assignment in a unique way. "I would give him a composer, say, Mozart, Chopin or Beethoven, and he would then come back and say that was like a punch 9-iron—all depending on the tone and the tempo of the classical music," said Mary Mickelson. Mickelson's response was typical of the way he referenced everything he did by the sport.

"I can remember meeting with the teachers on teacher day," said Mary. "They said Phil liked to sit and stare at the floor, and they couldn't figure out why." Philip's explanation to his demand-ing parent was simple enough. Mickelson said, "I was staring at the ground because I was trying to figure out which way a golf ball would roll. Would it break to the left or to the right?"

The high school music appreciation class took hold when Phil bought his Scottsdale Condominium. His boyish innocence was evident when he recently told his mother, "I wish I had taken piano lessons." Neither Phil nor Amy can play the baby grand piano that sits in their living room. "I was so surprised to hear Philip regretted not taking piano," said his mother. The nice thing about the Mickelsons' state-of-the-art baby grand is that they do not need to know how to play it. They insert a disk, and it plays itself. Mickelson is the only PGA Tour millennium kid with a high-tech piano.

A typical scholastic day for the golf-minded student-ath-lete was to attend classes, and then, as soon as the bell rang for the end of school, he would trek up the hill to the Stardust Golf Course. When it got dark, he would stand patiently at the main-tenance shed, waiting for his mother to pick him up. It was early in his days at University of San Diego High School that Phil gave his parents a scare. "We were so worried about Philip's direction, we looked into taking a Dobbins class on his behavior," said Mary. The Mickelsons were trying to find a way to discipline their son without breaking his spirit. "We wanted to control Philip, but he often had his own direction," said his mother.

At one point, Philip would say, "I'm not going to go to college because I'm going to make golf my living." His parents tried to reinforce the importance of an education by ignoring his sentiment. They would say, "So, Philip, what do want to major in when you get to college?"

A few months passed, and Mary Mickelson picked her son up at Stardust one summer day. He climbed into the backseat and broke the silence with, "I just want you to know, Mom, I'm going to go to college, and I am going to be majoring in business." Mary Mickelson just shook her head with a calm acceptance. She kept the car on the road, but was amazed at Philip's epiphany. She did not figure out until recently that Philip had played with a young man from Los Angeles who was schooled at Princeton. He told the gifted young left-hander from San Diego, "With your game, you better go to college and major in business, because you're going to make a lot of money, and you'd better know what you're going to do with all of it."

SUMMER VACATION

Like any growing family, the daily routine was often a struggle. Mickelson family vacations were one way to break away from the stress and routine of school, golf Tournaments, and long days at the nearby retirement center.

The Mickelsons liked to escape their own backyard and seek enjoyment in a non-golf environment. In the mid-1980s, the Mickelsons ventured to Lake Shasta, California's largest man-made lake located in Northern California. The Mickelsons decided to rent a houseboat and enjoy the scenery and water sports that gave the lake a reputation for being an aquatic refuge for the whole family.

The idea of a trip the week before a major junior Tournament bothered the finely tuned junior player. Not being around a course or his own backyard would be torture. His golfer's intuition told him that somehow he could find a way to practice. The thought of lounging around on a rented houseboat in the middle of Lake Shasta with his family was almost sinister to Philip. Maybe, he could just forget about the game for a week?

Philip considered the impending vacation the same way he mirrored his dad's golf swing—he improvised. The rented houseboat had a flat top, where the Mickelson kids could sunbathe during the day and sleep at night time, but Philip did not want to spend his time sunbathing. He decided to turn the top of the house boat into a Wiffle-ball driving range.

When the family finally went on vacation, he managed to sneak a packet of plastic Wiffle balls and a couple of irons onto the houseboat so that he could defy the windy conditions and drive Wiffle balls, almost 40 feet, into Lake Shasta. Phil's brother Tim would be the human ball retriever on a jet-ski. This plan worked well until Tim decided he had enough of being the retriever, and would said, "That's it, Philip, I'm done."

Philip would reply, "No, no Timmy, just one more time."

With his younger brother abandoning the role of the aquatic whiffle shagger, Philip would then get in the Jet-Ski and retrieve his own whiffle balls. It doesn't get much better than eight to 10 Wiffle balls on the top of a houseboat in the middle of Lake Shasta. So much for the quiet Mickelson aquatic-family vacation. Phil Sr. and Mary Mickelson just shook their heads, not being able to escape the sport for even a couple days in the middle of Lake Shasta. Although Philip devised a plan to get his club and the Wiffle balls onto the houseboat, one thing he did forget was a strip of Astroturf.

"When we brought the houseboat back, we were unloading it and we had to walk up this ramp to unload. As we were coming down the ramp, we could see the top of the houseboat and all these scrapes. I looked at Phil and said, 'If the rental people look up there, oh my gosh, we've had it,'" said Mary.

Later that same summer, the imposing nature of the golf course was an enticing lure to the 15-year-old. Having not completed household chores for an impending planned family gathering, Philip was ushered to his room until dinner. That's where he decided to pull a Mickelsonian. As the meal was about to be served, Mary and Phil Sr. went up to invite their oldest son back to the dinner table. He was not in his room, but there was evidence of a window departure. The Mickelsons went back down stairs and told their guests to enjoy the prepared meal and they would be right back. When they got to Stardust, they climbed on a cart and headed out on a search for their son. They had a hunch he was trying to get in nine holes before dark.

Mickelson got in about seven holes before his parents showed up in the golf cart.

He commented to his playing partners, "Thank you very much, I've enjoyed this." Then he put his bag on the cart, climbed in and nobody ever said a word until they got back to the house. Phil admitted later that he paid his neighbor five dollars to take him to the course.

Gamesmanship and games were also a part of the Mickelsonian junior reign. At Otter Creek Golf Club, in Columbus, Indiana, Mickelson was hitting balls from divots on the range. There was not a lot to do in Columbus, Indiana. In fact, the options were limited to two—picking corn or playing golf at one of the finest public courses in America. On this particular Tuesday in 1987, Mickelson chose the latter. Just as he had done in his backyard in San Diego, Mickelson would carve the earth with his clubs to manufacture new shots. Flopping a divot over the ball and chopping it out was plain "fun." He was prone to the inventive side.

"The one thing about Mickelson is, from an outward appearance you would underestimate him. He was dumb as a fox," said AJGA director Hamblin. As Mickelson was foddering on the range, the local Otter Creek junior club champion approached, looking for a three-hole game. Mickelson was the second player the young man approached. "Want to play a few holes?" he asked.

"Nah, I just want to practice," said Mickelson.

The club champion pestered, "Come on, I'll make it worth your effort. We'll play $5 a hole." Mickelson grudgingly agreed to play and proceeded to play the three holes birdie, birdie, birdie. Walking back to the clubhouse, the young hometown shark, looking bitten, said, "I know who you are. You're the left-hander I read about in the paper." Mickelson went on to win the AJGA Midwestern Junior.

It could be said Mickelson played too much junior golf, but that's like telling Michelangelo he spent too much time sculpting marble. When he had a chance to play in amateur events, specifically in the summer of 1988, he opted for junior competition. Why? "Because that's where my friends were," he would say. Mickelson's demeanor and candor were always applauded. Before Chris Haack gravitated to college golf at Georgia, he served as foundation director for the American Junior Golf Association. He also served as a pseudo big brother to the pack of golf bag-toting juniors. He reminded everyone, "You'd hear kids were jealous of Phil and his game. But Phil used his game as a way to communicate." He added, "Phil was so genuinely nice and polite, he had some people fooled into thinking it was all a big show."

Occasionally, Mickelson would transcend gamesmanship to enter the arena of showmanship. In 1987, at the Flint Elks Lodge 222 course in Flint, Michigan, Mickelson was one shot off the lead, heading to the 18th hole of the AJGA Great Lakes Buick Junior. Flint Elks Lodge was the home course for a strong junior program developed by one-time AJGA administrator Steve Braun. Flint has largely been heralded as a hotbed for basketball and football prospects, but one week each summer, the best junior golfers play in the national event. It has become a cornerstone on the AJGA calendar because of its strength of field, not for the course. It was a traditional course, but the lack of an adequate irrigation system made its appearance more of a links style.

On the 18th hole, Mickelson needed a birdie to get into a playoff. The prospect of getting into the playoff looked bleak when he pulled his approach shot to the left of the green. Close to 150 people gathered around as Mickleson surveyed the situation. He was approximately 20 yards from the green, which sloped away from him. The shot called for him to hit a high flop shot and let the ball flow to the hole. Mickelson was obviously his own caddie, but aware that he had a increasing number of interested spectators, he motioned for a young boy to take the pin out of the hole. The little boy scurried across the green, grabbed the pin with two hands, and pulled the flagstick out. Mickelson, with his collar flipped up, made a final presidential stroll up to the green. After a few full practice swings, he hit a flop shot that flew softly out of the thin, dry rough surrounding the green. As it rolled in the cup, he smiled that familiar California grin. He had tied for the lead.

He eventually beat Bill Heim and Jerry Houchnell on the second playoff hole to win. Call it a flair for the dramatic: Mickelson never missed an opportunity to drop a spectator's jaw, whether it was by skipping a ball off a lake to a tucked pin or punching a 9-iron with enough spin to cause it to track from the back of the green to the front.

During his days on the kids' circuit, Mickelson rarely wore hats or visors from junior golf to his early days on the PGA Tour. A very noticeable piece of equipment, hats are relied upon by companies for product identification. Mickelson, never one to consider even a white bucket hat as part of his equipment, has always had a disdain for headwear. Steve Loy and Yonex helped convince him that a visor and a long-term endorsement contract looked pretty good.

When Harry Met Philip
(Junior Golf to the College Years)

Although they did not know it at the time, the same Harry Rudolph whom Mickelson met as a six-year-old would come to be one of Philip's fiercest competitors in junior, and later, college golf. "I think we both fed off of each other, said Rudolph. "If he won and I didn't, I was upset. I'm sure there was some of that same fire in him."

They pushed each other on the golf course. As they grew to be young men, their games evolved as well. Phil Sr. reflected, "Phil was good for Harry and Harry was good for Phil." Rudolph is six months older than Mickelson and what happened between them is a full-circle irony of sorts. As six-year-olds, the two would play the San Diego par-3 course, Presidio Hills. They ended up going to rival high schools, Mickelson to the University of San Diego High School and Rudolph to La Jolla High School. They traveled thousands of miles from the San Diego area to compete in national junior and amateur competitions, only to compete again against each other, in AJGA competition and USGA and other amateur events.

In 1988, the two high school seniors were considered the top two NCAA recruits in the country. Both were considering Arizona State University. At the time, Arizona State head coach Steve Loy had only one scholarship available. Rudolph made his decision first, choosing to attend Oklahoma State, where Mike Holder had established the top program in the nation. Mickelson opted for Arizona State, where the Sun Devils were in the process of building an on-campus Pete Dye-designed golf course. Mary Mickelson remembers doing some coaching of her own for Steve Loy, even before her son went to Arizona State. "Steve," she said, "Philip will really do anything you want him to do; it just depends on how you ask him."

Rudolph had a disdain for Mickelson's game on the course. "He definitely liked to play mind games, and, I don't know, maybe that's what made him a great player. As far back as I can remember, even in college, he would be a jokester, prankster type, but our battles on the golf course got real quiet when I was in college," said Rudolph.

Rudolph left the Oklahoma State program after two-and-a-half years because, he said, "My game was not getting any better." He wound up at the University of Arizona, the main rival to Arizona State and team Steve Loy and Phil Mickelson.

At Arizona, Rick LaRose had compiled a competitive team. With Jim Furyk, David Berganio, Manny Zerman (Mickelson's high school teammate, senior prom double-date partner and later his rival in the finals of the 1990 U.S. Amateur) and now Rudolph, the Wildcats became national contenders. Mickelson won his three NCAA individual titles in 1989, 1990 and 1992, and the Sun Devils won the team championship at Innisbrook in Tarpon Springs, Florida, in 1990, on the same course where Mickelson chased squirrels while playing junior golf at the American Junior Classic. This time, Mickelson chased the Florida Gators in the final round, as his team rallied from 11 strokes back on the final day to claim the national championship by two strokes.

Rudolph did not get revenge on Mickelson until 1992, when his Arizona team won the NCAA championship. Playing with Mickelson the last two rounds, Rudolph again was cast into the foreground with his old foe.

The two, who as six-year-olds, learned the game together, finally took divergent cart paths. Mickelson leapfrogged Q-school to the green-lined fairways of the PGA Tour, and Rudolph was headed for the hardship of the Nike Tour and eventually the Asian Tour. While Phil's game matured onto the PGA Tour, Rudolph attempted to climb the minor league ladder. There he found the frustrations of a different game.

"The cutthroat thing about the Nike Tour is, you were paying the same amount to travel as you would on the PGA Tour, to play for 10-tenth the amount of money. You could shoot ten under-par and make $900. Then you added up your expenses and were in the hole four hundred dollars that week," "Rudolph said. He added, "You'd finish grinding your butt off and you just shot some great scores and you'd come in and laugh. I just broke even."

While Rudolph was hitting the wall of economics on the Nike Tour, Mickelson was a world away. On the surface, the Nike Tour was just one step away from the PGA Tour, but as Rudolph realized, it was really a totally different game. "If you had a choice to layup or go for it in any Nike event, you'd go for it, because what's par going to get you?"

While both he and Mickelson refined their games, they did so in different realms. "Look at his backyard. That's why he was such a wizard around the greens. The rest of the time, I suspect, Phil was at Stardust or playing in Tournaments," said Rudolph.

Rudolph observed the Mickelsonian run with admiration. The Tournaments he claimed from 1989 to 1991 echo a can anyone ever top-this list. Harry Rudolph guessed, "I always figured by the Tournaments that Phil won, it was like he had a list and just went through it, checking them off." Rudolph admired Mickelson's recognition of the history of the game: "He knew the history of especially amateur golf and would set the bar pretty high. I think that was as much of a driving force for him as anything."

When he arrived at Arizona State, it didn't take long for Mickelson to show his game. Jim Brown, longtime coach at Ohio State, remembers Mickelson's college dominance. "We got the opportunity to play with Arizona State a lot," "In all my years of college coaching, he was the best. When he was chipping and putting, the ball was always on the hole. When it didn't go in, it burned the edge. Every hole. I was disappointed it didn't go in every time."

Mickelson burned the edge off the course, too. While studying in his off-campus apartment for a test, Mickelson was in need of some extra lighting. He pulled a nearby table lamp onto the couch. About an hour later his roommates smelled smoke. The lamp had burned a small hole in the couch where he was studying. The trio of golfers escaped a small apartment fire, but the rest of the NCAA Division I programs did not escape the left-hander's dominance. In 1991, Warren Schutte (pronounced SCUTTA) of UNLV interrupted what could have been an unprecedented four straight NCAA individual titles. Mickelson was playing college golf, but he was really playing a different game from the other NCAA Division I schools. When Charles Barkley called (then playing for the Phoenix Suns) for a game, he realized he was out of golf balls. Both of his roommates, Rob Mangini and Trip Kuehne, knew they would have to build a fortress around their reserves. It didn't matter, Mickelson somehow found Kuehne's stash. His magic was ubiquitous. He had a way to accomplish what he needed on the course and away from the course. "He had an uncanny ability to, if there was a Tournament he wanted to win, he was able to win it," said Kuehne, who eventually transferred from Arizona State to Oklahoma State. And with Mickelson, a win on the fairways usually meant the Sun Devils would end up at Anderson's in Tempe to celebrate the win.

Mickelson was writing papers at Arizona State and rewriting record books. His 1989 and 1990 NCAA individual championships were followed by winning the 1990 U.S. Amateur. Then, in 1991, he started the second-semester of his junior year at Arizona State by claiming the Northern Telecom Open. At the age of 20, Mickelson's could see that his day on the PGA Tour was dawning. Winning as an amateur put him in a class with names like Frances Ouimet, Gene Sarazen and Ray Floyd. He would say, "Gosh, I'm fortunate to have the opportunity to compete." Mickelson went from a great college golfer at Arizona State to having Charles Barkley calling him for a game, from playing with Michael Jordan in the Western Amateur to three of golf's four majors in 1991.

To say life is cyclical would be a cliché. To say golf is cyclical would be too general, but in 1991 the forces of parallelism met head-on at Hazeltine Golf Course in Minnesota for Mickelson's first appearance in the event. Born on June 16, 1970, Mickelson was just a couple of days old when they played the first-ever U.S. Open at Hazeltine. And 21 years later, his birthday fell on the third round (Saturday). Mickelson, like Crenshaw in 1970, was the best amateur in the game. And he already had a PGA TOUR victory in his back pocket. At Hazeltine, he finished tied for 55th, as a 34-year-old named Payne Stewart beat Scott Simpson in an 18-hole playoff on Monday. A young caddie named Jim Mackay was Simpson's caddie at Hazeltine. And Mackay, nicknamed "Bones," would send a letter less than a year later to Mickelson, who turned pro in June of 1992, to offer his services. The letter marked the birth of a team that still exists today.

FROM WALKING TO RYDING

Between Mickelson's junior highlights and his PGA Tour heroics, he sandwiched two appearances on the prestigious Walker Cup team (1989 and 1991) by winning the U.S. Amateur in 1990. His undefeated (3-0-1) Walker Cup singles aided the U.S. win in 1991. Mickelson's match play, record in the early 1990s was phenomenal. "With match-play the anxiety is knowing who you are playing, but not what you have to shoot. That is the same anxiety to deal with, whether it's your first match or your fourth," said Mickelson. The U.S. lost by a single point (12 1/2 - 11 1/2) in 1989, Mickelson's first Walker Cup appearance.

The makeup of the 1991 U.S. team, that defeated the European effort 14-10, was interesting. Driving-range owner-turned-Senior PGA player, Allen Doyle, and longtime Pennsylvania amateur Jay Sigel represented the experienced side of the team. Mickelson, Mike Sposa, David Duval, Bob May, and Tom Scherrer gave the team youthful exuberance.

Mickelson followed up his impressive match-play record from 1989 to 1991 (9-0-1) in the national amateur and Walker Cups with a spot on the 1995 Ryder Cup team at Oak Hill Country Club. Captain Lanny Wadkins excused Mickelson's amateur match-play success with a shrug. The first of the 20-something quartet to make a Ryder Cup team, Mickelson surprised everyone in Rochester with a 3-0-0 match record. He downed his former Sun Devil teammate Per Ulrik Johansson in singles (2 and 1). He teamed with Corey Pavin to down Johansson and Bernhard Langer (6 and 4) in one fourball match, and he combined with Jay Haas to top one of his childhood icons, Seve Ballesteros, playing with David Gilford, (3 and 2) in another.

Wadkins was so pleased with Mickelson's match-play efforts that he second-guessed his decision to use the left-hander in foursome play. Could Mickelson in foursome play have been the counterbalance to retain the cup? Curtis Strange lost his singles match by bogeying the final three holes. The one-point loss (14 1/2 - 13 1/2) on American soil hurt the pride of the U.S. team. The memory of the closing ceremony still haunts Wadkins, and is one that Mickelson will take with him in future competitions.

In 1997, the U.S. assembled a much younger team than the one at Oak Hill. Justin Leonard, Tiger Woods and Jim Furyk were Ryder Cup rookies. Mickelson was a Ryder Cup veteran, according to captain Tom Kite. On the course, the U.S. was getting off to a terrible start, 5-3. The 20-something group was up against young European players like Lee Westwood, Thomas Bjorn and Ignacio ("Nacho") Garrido. Mickelson, playing with Davis Love III, lost a close match to José Maria Olazabal and Costantino Rocca 1-up in four-ball competition on Day 1. Kite paired Mickelson with Tom Lehman for the foursome and four-ball matches. They halved both of their matches.

After defeating Darren Clarke 2 and 1 in singles, Mickelson owned a impressive (4-1-2) Ryder Cup record. Following Saturday play, the Europeans needed just 3 1/2 points in singles play to keep the cup. Kite and former president George Bush tried to rally the young American team, but the deficit was too large. The U.S. would eventually leave Spain without the Ryder Cup, losing 14 1/2 - 13 1/2. Mickelson's dominating record in match play took a small hit, but to Mickelson, records were not the bane of his existence. From his U.S. Amateur title at Cherry Hills to Brookline for his third Ryder Cup, Mickelson's (13-1-2) record is impressive.

TOUR TODDLER

Now a sophomore on the PGA Tour, Mickleson has won 13 Tour events since he first put a peg in the ground in Tour soil in 1992. Nick Price, with 15, is the only player to capture more titles, but it's his 0-for streak in the majors, which his longtime caddie Jim Mackay and Mickelson carry down every fairway like it's an additional endorsement deal. Having a bag tag like the best player never to win a major would be a heavy burden to some. Not Mickelson. After all, his 13 wins also put him close to the top 50 all-time Tour winners in the game, just a few wins shy of names like Tom Weiskopf (15), Curtis Strange (17), and Jack Burke (17). Lurking at 18 wins is Greg Norman.

Success to some is a green jacket and claret jug, but the righthanded lefty refuses to buckle. He's enjoying being a pretty famous father and he's in no hurry. "Sure, I am somewhat frustrated none of my wins have come in a major, but, I don't think it's unfair," and Mickelson's mind trails to his next task at hand. Just as he was focused, for his first NCAA championship, Mickelson is ready for the prime of his career. "I don't want to win just one," said Mickelson who was almost the little putter boy that could at Pinehurst. He came away with more than a trophy, Amanda, the little putter girl.

Many of the PGA Tour veterans consider Mickelson the most settled of all the 20-something players. His agent, Steve Loy of Cornerstone Sports, is the same man who recruited him for Arizona State University in 1988. His wife, Amy, the taskmaster away from the course, oversees his travel plans, gym workouts and anything else that is an obstacle to his on-course concentration.

Could Mickelson be too comfortable and settled to have a fiery attitude about winning a major? As an amateur, was the competition too weak for Mickelson? The win allowed him to skip Q-school and head from the deserts of Arizona to the broiler of the PGA Tour. Instead of being just an amateur with a wry smile who stands on the wrong side of the ball, Mickelson quickly became the next "can't-miss kid"—the next Nicklaus. After all, Mickelson was the first player (1990) since the blond slugger from Ohio State to claim a rare double (NCAA and U.S. Amateur) in 1961.

The Mickelsonian era had started on the PGA Tour. The clock was ticking, and few could control its heart-pounding resonance. This also meant that the San Diego native was devoid of a rookie grace-and-adjustment period on the big-boy Tour. Winning a PGA Tour event as an amateur was like wearing a siren hat down the fairways. The PGA Tour veterans didn't care if they saw the sultan of southpaws tee it up in the "big's."

This was obviously a different league, but unlike other sports, the transition to professional golf from an equipment and course standpoint does not scare too many. It's adding millions of dollars in prize money, galleries, a media frenzy and agent hassles, which provide a little adrenaline. Throw in qualification standards for Ryder Cups, President's Cups and now world championships, and the hunt is on.

Taking a look at the prize money since Mickelson joined the Tour in 1992, would make a stockbroker's knees quiver. In 1992, the 44 events had combined total purse of less than $50 million. On the eve of the next millennium, the figure stands at close to $150 million. The money has changed the game. Consider that when Mickelson was born, in 1970, Lee Trevino was the leading money winner with $157,037.63. This is about the same amount the third-place finisher would win today in the 1999 Greater Milwaukee Open.

Warm-ups have never really been Mickelson's thing. Take, for instance, his record in the month of January on the PGA Tour. The Northern Telecom (1991)—January; the Buick Invitational (1993)—January; the Mercedes Championship (1994)—January; the Northern Telecom (1995)—January, the Nortel Open (1996); the Phoenix Open (1996)—January; the Mercedes Championship (1998)—January. Only a hard rain kept him from adding to his total in the month of January in 1998. The AT&T Pebble Beach National Pro-Am's final round was postponed until August in 1998. Overall, seven of Mickelson's 13 wins have come in the first month. Four times (1994, 1995, 1996, 1998) he has been named the PGA Tour Player of the Month for January. Either the west coast courses, grass, playing conditions, or home-cooking explain his early season success.

The Bay Hill Invitational remains his only PGA Tour win east of the Mississippi. For some reason, the PGA Tour doesn't recognize Mickelson's key junior wins (1987 and 1988) at the Great Lakes Buick at Flint Elks Lodge 222 in Flint, Michigan, or his Midwestern Junior win at Otter Creek in Columbus, Indiana.

THE MICKELSON FLOP

In 1994, trying to come of age on the PGA Tour, Mickelson decided to head to Flagstaff for a ski outing with college friends Jim Strickland and Rob Mangini. Mickelson's style on the slopes and his greenside play are synonymous. His effortless style gives the impression that he was born to do both. Only a race to the bottom of the hill left Mickelson in a tangled mess, that resulted in a broken femur and ankle. His 1994 PGA Tour campaign was derailed by snow and ice.

THROUGH THE LOOKING GLASS

Both Phil and Mary Mickelson have shared the frustrations of following their son on Tour. Mary went to such lengths as imitating a PGA Tour statistician to get inside the ropes for a closer look at her son. This lasted a short while, until Charlie Jones, doing PGA Tour radio broadcasts, decided to divulge the identity of the phony statistician on the air. "I had a clipboard and visor and was just roaming the course, writing down numbers, but it didn't work," said Mary.

With their frustration heightened by Philip's PGA Tour success in 1996 and their inability to watch him play, Mary went looking for the perfect gift for her husband. She ended up traveling to the San Francisco area for a Tournament that Phil's dad was unable to attend. Roaming the fairways, battling the galleries, Mary was again trying to get a glimpse of her son. She came upon a man standing stationary, looking through what she described as a "long, pencil-thin periscope." At the time, her husband, Phil, was carrying a step stool and binoculars. She quickly learned where she could purchase the periscope and wrapped it up for her husband's Christmas present in 1996.

Phil was taken with the new apparatus and discovered its benefits: it gives binocular vision as if an average-height adult is almost eight feet tall. As he began to use the periscope at PGA Tour events, many eyes turned from Philip Alfred Mickelson on the fairway, toward Philip Anthony Mickelson, the proud father with a toy. So many of his friends, some parents of other PGA Tour players envied his newfound vision. He quickly ordered 15 of the periscopes for his friends. His large order also led him to a conversation with the periscope's inventor, George Miller. Miller, 79, had a bout with cancer and was frustrated trying to continue the marketing efforts for his periscope, which had military, security surveillance, and no sports applications. This prompted Miller to approach Mickelson with an attractive business offer. As they had with the Mickelson backyard 25 years before, Phil and Mary Mickleson saw an opportunity with a price tag.

Phil said, "George told me, 'I'll sell my business to you if you promise me one thing—make them available to as many contacts as possible.'" Miller sold Mickelson on the concept and the business. A deal was struck. Mickelson received the patents, trademarks, and Miller's remaining inventory (approximately 1,100 units).

His first step was to improve the periscope. "I quickly approached the PGA and USGA. I also wanted to get a stamp of approval on the use of the devices at the different events," said the new business owner. He maintained the military and law-enforcement accounts, but his primary focus was on the sport of golf. While the military and law-enforcement officials used the periscope for surveillance, it was the "new" application that Mickelson wanted to foster.

As galleries have continued to grow on the PGA Tour, so has the need to be able to see the action. The wide paper box with dual mirrors, which was developed in the late 1960s, was banned at most events because it impeded the view of others in the gallery. "You get three or four of those boxes, and it's like a brick wall," said Mickelson. In just over three years, Mickelson received approval for his "pencil-thin" periscope, newly named the "Sportscope," which contains a series of five lenses. A prism on the bottom of the scope allows the viewer to adjust the focus.

Augusta is the only Tournament that has not yet allowed the Sportscope. Henry Hughes of the PGA and Judy Bell of the USGA worked closely with Mickelson to grant their organizations' stamps of approval in time for the Sportscope's international debut at the 1997 Ryder Cup matches at Valderrama. Making the trip were 1,400 Sportscopes and their captain, Phil Mickelson Sr. This was a nervous time for "big" Phil, and not because his son again represented the U.S. Before the first group made the turn, Mickelson's elevated eye was a hit. More than 1,050 were springing up throughout the course in less than an hour and a half. Then, the Sportscope leader came upon a frightening realization. "As I did a quick inventory, I realized I was missing about 350 units," said Mickelson. "Here was a throng of Spanish fans wanting to purchase Sportscopes, and I was literally out of them the first day." A quick survey of shipping labels and he met head-on with customs officials. When Mickelson finally tracked the missing units to customs, his conversation was brief. "No habla Español" was the beginning and the end.

THE MICKELSONIAN FLOP SHOT

In the opening round of the 1997 PGA at Winged Foot, Mickelson had an opportunity to execute the flop shot. Having missed the 16th green in the deep rough to the right, Phil Mickelson grabbed his lob wedge and opened the face. He was trying to put an exclamation point on what could be a strong opening round in a major. The club arched back and through with a fullness that is rarely seen around greenside play. The ball fluttered out, which made it appear like a Ping-Pong ball with wings, not a Titleist. The ball rolled gently to the hole, nestled against the pin for a brief moment and then toppled into the hole.

Following the round, Mickelson tried to explain the shot. "That particular shot," the humble left-hander said, "I felt if I could just hit that shot as soft as possible, I had a huge margin for error. But it wasn't that difficult to get it close. I was just awfully lucky that it went in."

It was the kind of floating flop shot that he hit in the first round of the 1997 PGA that typified Mickelson's game—a game defined by greenside finesse and graceful power. Mickelson length off PGA Tour tee boxes is deceptive. He's continually among the top 25 players in total driving distance, but his reputation was earned through wedge play.

University of Georgia golf coach Chris Haack, said, "Phil Mickelson was the first guy to try to actually hit a shot where it would go over your head and behind you. Kids on my team say, 'I'm going to hit the Mickelson shot.' He was so creative that he figured out a way to do things that you'd swear were not possible." The four words "small margin for error" are the best way to describe the lob shot. Whether the ball is buried in thick rough, or whether it's sitting up on a tightly cut collar or even the hard pan accustomed to links golf, the lob shot has been perfected by few at golf's defining level. Even at Arizona State, Mickelson required constant practice to perfect its execution. Mickelson and his Sun Devil roommates found a unique way to create an air-conditioned practice facility in their living room. Mickelson took the air conditioning vent off above the door frame and would hit lob shots into the vent.

In a made-for-cable production, PGA Tour Productions invited musician Kenny G and Mickelson to collaborate on a celebrity golf show at Mickelson's home course, Grayhawk, in Scottsdale in 1998. PGA Tour Productions' Brian Donovan remembers witnessing the Mickelsonian wedge. "He stood with his back to the green and pin and hit the ball and it actually landed behind him on the green." And Mickelson does not hesitate to hit the flop shot in competition. He likes to say the genesis of the shot was on Wenrich Road in San Diego—the Mickelson backyard.

> ## "An artist has to take life as he finds it. Life by itself is formless wherever it is. Art must give it form."
> ### —Hugh MacLenman

It must have happened long before Leroy Nieman, but there is no one quintessential comparative beginning between golf and the world of art. In 1972, Nick Seitz analyzed Neiman's impact on sports: "He has the journalistic talent, as well as the artistic ability, to convey the essence of a game or contestant with great impact." Sam Snead's swing would certainly foster a comparison between the two kingdoms of art and golf. And one of Neiman's most famous works features a collage of six great golf champions: Jack Nicklaus, Arnold Palmer, Lee Trevino, Gary Player, Ben

Hogan and Sam Snead. As he has done with so many sports, Neiman related golf through colors and forms that enveloped deeper meaning. The simple symmetry of the human body as it coils and then uncoils evinces a balance and introduces angles, important aspects of art.

In the world of sports, many athletes have exhibited qualities, in their respective sports, that conjure artistic comparisons. As they excel at their craft, their movements and the mode in which they accomplish their feats is extraordinary. Wayne Gretzky was not the strongest or even the fastest hockey player on the planet, yet he combined athletic instincts with ability. This combination led many to label him an "artist."

Greg Maddux, a finesse pitcher, does not rely on an overpowering fastball. Rather, he shapes the plate and batters with a precision that affords him success. The same goes for the now-retired Barry Sanders in the NFL. His maneuverability transcended power and entered an arena where he was considered da Vinci in turf shoes. Imagine. Within the barbaric sport of football, a sport that harbors similarities to trench warfare, could there be an artist? Phil Mickelson is a rare athlete who combines the power of driving a golf ball with an ability, an almost sixth sense, around the greens.

One thing Phil's father is quick to point out: "Phil's a right-hander, playing the game left-handed." Asked on Tour if his father ever tried to change him to a right-handed player Mickelson's response was a simple "Gosh, no sir."

**"IT IS WELL WITH ME ONLY WHEN
I HAVE A CHISEL IN MY HAND."
—MICHELANGELO**

Ambidexterity is the ability to efficiently command both hands to accomplish a task. And while Mickelson does simply everything but golf right-handed, it can successfully be argued that his abilities from the left and the right are not matched. It is interesting to note that Mickelson's brother Tim is a left-hander, but he plays golf right-handed.

Delving past the ambidextrous surface of history leads us to artists like Michelangelo and Leonardo da Vinci. Could Mickelson's touch around the green be similar to the precision sculptures of the great Florentine artist Michelangelo? Take the art of putting and chipping as a separate genre from the basic golf swing. The lack of movement of the lower body is isolated. The extremities are also limited, and the hand and arm movements, along with precision hand-eye coordination, determine a successful touch.

Mary Mickelson insists her son was "never very artistic." But is Mickelson turning a game of millimeters into an art form? The basic premise is that the right brain controls the left side of the body, and the left brain controls the right side of the body. Mickelson's right brain bears his creativity. Take, for example, the home run power of Ken Griffey Jr. and Mark McGwire. Both excel at the same craft, except McGwire's home runs could be tagged "right-handed power" and Griffey's "left-handed grace." These simple functions from opposite sides of the plate separate the balance. To bring the comparison to the green: Corey Pavin executes delicate shots around the green like a tactician. Mickelson's form is more like a brush stroke. Mickelson's swing developed from a visual perception of watching his father swing right-handed.

While Mickelson has full command of his artful game, the PGA Tour does not award prize money on the strength of a perfect swing plane—art can easily be ignored. As Mickelson kept winning PGA events, the BPNTWAM (best player never to win a major) label was starting to catch up with his mind. And in the 1990s on the PGA Tour, sports psychologists were the norm. After all, Mickelson had his former college coach as his agent, he had a supportive family, and success seemed to follow.

Bob Rotella came on the scene last year when Mickelson decided he needed to approach course management a little differently. Seeing the success of David Duval, Justin Leonard, and most of all, Tiger Woods, was reason enough that he needed to address his mental approach to the game. Firing at closely guarded pins on par-3s and abandoning practice on his short game were catching up with him.

Rotella had earned a solid reputation for working with Davis Love, Hal Sutton, Brad Faxon, and close to 20 other PGA players. Mickelson was always the player in command at the junior and amateur levels. Now, under the scrutiny of millions, a small amount of doubt had entered his head. Rotella emphasized the importance of players "staying in the present," meaning not letting past or future shots dictate their game plan. He also sought out longtime PGA professional Jack Burke in Houston to evaluate his swing and short game.

Mickelson had worked with Dean Reinmuth since the age of 14, but their relationship spoiled during Mickelson's early days on the PGA Tour. Like any expectant father, Mickelson weighed life's "in the present" burdens. Baby on the way, fitness, mental approach to the game.

About this same time, Mickelson's caddie Jim Mackay (Bones) was getting a lot of ink. *Golf Digest* had run a story about caddies, and it had drawn more attention to the monetary gains afforded the loopers. The Islesworth neighbors O'Meara and Woods, both let their caddies (Jerry Higginbotham and Mike "Fluff" Cowan) go for various reasons. The veritable *Caddyshack* on Tour was beginning to look like the fictional one at Bushwood and not the PGA Tour. Mackay was not about to be let go. From appearances, one of team Mickelson's strengths was Mackay, a comrade who had Phil's best interests in mind.

The tutelage provided by Mickelson's parents was always a support system designed to help him understand the importance of the person—he would return home from a semester at Arizona State and gingerly escape his Honda CVC hatchback, which was just a little bigger than a golf cart, and kiddingly greet his mom in the kitchen with "The great one is home." His mother would bristle at the comment and add, "The success you've had in golf does not make you the person." Both parents would constantly remind Philip that golf was an opportunity. He would test his parents' patience the same way he would burn the rim of the cup in the backyard.

The extent of the mischievous side of Phillip growing up was a trip to Tijuana to help a friend who was trying to get across the border but did not have his credentials. The customs officials were threatening to keep him until he could prove verification. At the time, Phil was told not to leave the Mickelson house. "Phil really didn't get in trouble, but he went to Tijuana when he wasn't supposed to," said his father. When Mickelson returned home late that night, he realized he would have to pay the price of sleeping on the front stoop. The door was locked. The friend he rescued from customs officials turned out to be Manny Zerman, the same young man Mickelson defeated to win the 1990 U.S. Amateur in Colorado.

Compared to the other 20-something players, Mickelson is as grounded as they come. Brad Faxon said, "Phil's more mature than a lot of the young players on Tour." A settled family man, in April he was 11th in the Ryder Cup standings and stayed away from the Tour. It wasn't that he did not want to be part of the U.S. effort at Brookline, but his family came first. "People think it's sick that I am so nice to Amy, but I think it is important," he said. Earnings of $6 million since he turned pro in 1992 and his first child due in June are good excuses not to play in events like the Houston Open.

THE LITTLE PUTTER GIRL

In January at the Phoenix Open, Amy Mickelson, just three months' pregnant, helped organize a fund-raiser for children's charities. The rockin' '70s event, titled "Boogie Nights," featured a group of PGA Tour players representing the Village People. There was Mickelson (the construction worker) and Payne Stewart (the Indian); Billy Mayfair (the Sailor); Paul Azinger (the Cowboy); and Mark Calcavecchia (the Policeman). Mickelson and Stewart were just two rock-and-roll wannabes dancing, singing and gyrating to "YMCA" to give some children a second chance in life.

Mickelson, Mr. January on the PGA Tour, was playing in just his second event of the year at Phoenix. A dismal final- round 80 left him in 61st place. As a former champion (1996) Mickelson's first two final rounds of the year, a 78 at the Mercedes and the 80 at Phoenix were not indicative of his solid play. A few months later, the usually solid Mickelson was again sliding down the scoring chart. At the Players' Championship, he skidded to an 82. He played well at the Bell South and at Augusta, garnering top 10 finishes, but the PGA Tour statistics revealed that Mickelson's usually impeccable short game had escaped the left-hander. He was 133rd on for his ability to convert missing the green in regulation into pars, and he was 144th on Tour, averaging 74.33 strokes in the final round. It was an irony of sorts that his game off the tee boxes was his strength. With Amy's troubled pregnancy (she went into premature labor in March) and his agent not knowing if he would compete in another major until the

British Open at Carnoustie, Mickelson contemplated life's priorities.

The U.S. Open would be played at Pinehurst No. 2, a course that the players on Tour said would favor a player who could get up and down from anywhere. And that was Mickelson's game. Even though he did not come out in 1999 like he normally did and dominate in January, he still had the confidence to compete, especially around the green.

Jack Burke would give him swing tips that he would write down and study. It was an intuitive skill that just needed a little more rehearsal—like when he practiced in the backyard. He remembers the patience of his father, the time they spent together, hitting balls until dark. He remembers chipping contests with his brother Tim and the emotions of the playground evoking an indescribable feeling . . .

. . . Like the feeling when you hold your first child. Seven-pound, four-ounce Amanda Brynn Mickelson entered the world on June 21, 1999, one day after Father's Day and five days after Dad's 29th birthday. It will be a couple years before she can sit in her dad's lap and hear about how he tried to bring home a trophy the day before she was born. He will describe the fable about the old guy (a tortoise in knickers) who just barely beat the young heir (apparent) to the finish line. Her mom will probably say something like, "Dad talked about you all week." Amanda Mickelson will likely hear stories about her dad, who was willed into contention by his respect for the institution of fatherhood. She will probably hear dad say he pulled the putt on 17 (the 71st hole) because he thought the beeper was going off. She will probably hear a different version from the one witnessed by the golfing mainstream. When the championship was over, Mickelson did admit, "It would have made for a cool story for my daughter to read about as she got older."

Phil Mickelson knew long before Amanda was born that there are moments in life more important than a golf Tournament. The golf world couldn't shake the notion that he would drop his Scotty Cameron putter on the green and walk off the course had he received word Amanda was on her way. "I'm out of here. No decisions," he said again and again. But, what if you're on the range, as opposed to the 8th hole, as opposed to the 18th fairway? "I'm outta here. There will be a U.S. Open every year," he would say.

Mickelson shared his personal life with everyone. Something as private as a couple's first child was gallery gossip, headline text in major newspapers across America and noted long after the last gallery rope was ripped out of the Carolina sand.

What Mickleson accomplished in central North Carolina is a lot like what Donald Ross did at the turn of the 20th century. He creatively carved a niche. His stance, swing, and comments all week were Mickelsonian. Mickelson shed his image as the best player never to win a major (BPNTWAM) by finishing second. He said, "I took a chance of coming across the country to play. But I didn't come for a top-5 or top-10 finish, I came to win."

It is ironic to imagine the circle of emotions surrounding Mickelson's five and a half days at Pinehurst. His first- and second-round pairing a year earlier at the Olympic Club had been widely chronicled. The USGA's David Fay and Tom Meeks had given Mickelson a B pairing with Jeff Maggert and Colin Montgomerie. Saying the USGA sought forgiveness for Mickelson's Thursday-Friday pairing at Pinehurst would be too harsh an affirmation, but somehow, Mickelson was paired with David Duval and Carlos Franco. Duval was the No. 1 player in the world, and Franco was one of the hottest European players. Mickelson was the junior golfer of the year in 1988. Duval was the boy of summer in 1989. They are about as far apart on the personality scale as Beaver Cleaver and Bart Simpson, but the competitive pairing served both Mickelson and Duval quite well as they charged out to identical rounds of 67-70. In the third round, the father-to-be was matched with another millennium kid with a game, Tiger Woods.

Mickelson said, "All week I felt if I played like I played in college, which is to stay around par and not try to do anything exceptional," said Mickelson. He had the same focus he had on the driving range at Oak Tree before he won his first NCAA title. He had the maturity to recognize the value of par. He knew the number of strokes it is supposed to take mortals to complete a hole.

Mickelson explained the divisiveness of par by saying, "Duval played the first eight holes 5-over and was five shots off the lead. He made up two shots by parring in." On Saturday Tom Meeks said, "I think even-par might be holding the trophy." Instead, even par was one 15-foot putt from holding the trophy. Par was flying five and a half hours on a private plane to be bedside while his wife delivered their first child.

In a twist of fate, Amy Mickelson went into labor Monday morning. Even par could have been Payne Stewart standing on the 11th tee at the playoff on Monday asking, "Where did Phil go?"

Mickelson was not the No. 1 (Duval) or two (Woods) world-ranked 20-something player making a Sunday run. He was the only player who put himself in position to win. It was because of his short game that he was able to navigate the convex Pinehurst greens like a sculptor with a chisel and the mind of a poet like Keats. It was almost destiny.

In January, Mickelson usually performed a victory dance at Phoenix, the Mercedes, or any of the west coast stops. Instead, in 1999, he a human pretzel, spelling "YMCA" with former Sun Devil and friend Mayfair, Calcavecchia, Azinger, and Stewart.

Just helping his wife raise funds for underprivileged kids. Five months later, Stewart was dancing with his caddie, Mike Hicks, and Mickelson was left to spell BPNTWAM by himself. Mickelson's life was in complete order, but he felt the cloud of disappointment one day before he felt the gift of Amanda's life. It happened at "just another golf Tournament."

It is incredible to think that Mickelson will some day be standing in his backyard, just like when he was a little boy. He might tell Amanda he learned about the importance of the word *family* in his own backyard. He might tell her about the first major he played in, the one at Hazeltine, when he made the cut (Stewart won that year, too), and then he will say something like "It was a good thing you were born on the Monday after the U.S. Open; I'll never miss a birthday." Then he will display the Mickelsonian grin and say, "Unless there is a playoff."

At Pinehurst, Mickelson was constantly reminded that he had not had much success on the PGA Tour east of the Mississippi. The media would press for a reason why his game didn't respond to the winds of Florida and the poa annua on greens in the mid-Atlantic. Rather than bring up his big win at the Flint Elks Lodge 222, Mickelson gave a Mickelsonian response of "I've never really given it much thought."

Mickelson always seemed comfortable on the golf course. The foundation of his junior game was a fluid golf swing. The flipped-up collar and boyish looks gave the impression that Phil Mickelson was born to play the game. "I have always been a feel player with some mechanics. But I am not trying to work too much on mechanics for the simple reason that I am trying to find that rhythm or that groove," said Mickelson. Thirteen wins on the PGA Tour before his 30th birthday is a pretty good start. Will fatherhood slow him down or propel him? Will he spend more time at home and concentrate on the majors in the new millennium?

Mickelson has been able to coach the weaknesses out of his game. He has always relied on his instincts to execute properly. He has also taken that approach in life. Mickelson personifies art in motion on the course. Away from the course, he manages the Mickelsonian smile and is as stubbornly independent as he was when he hit range ball after range ball in the pouring rain at Oak Tree in 1989.

MR. NICKLAUS

Woods, Duval, Leonard, and Mickelson know the comparisons are going to come. Their shots are like spheric missiles bombing the fiberglass flagsticks across the globe. And as they snare tournaments, and records, and add majors to their growing résumés, there will be one name that they will be measured against. Jack Nicklaus—call him Mr. Jack Nicklaus. Mr. Nicklaus has elevated more than just a game for the young players on the PGA Tour.

He has set the table, sent out the invitations and iced the beverages. He has not done this alone, but what Nicklaus has cultivated will take more to undo than asking where Ryder Cup proceeds are heading, firing "Fluff" Cowan, yelling at the galleries for picture taking or dissing the media. Nicklaus was a gentleman's player who took the course and the competition one stroke at a time. He kept his family with him every step of the way, and his passion for the game spans generations.

In 1998, Nicklaus showed up at the Masters with six green sport jackets and a bad left hip. At 58, the old Nicklaus was looking like the venerable Nicklaus of old.

It was Tiger Woods who reminded everyone at the event that people reach their optimum physical capacity at age 28, then slowly lose one percent of their motor skills per year if they don't stay fit. Nicklaus didn't remind Woods that Nicklaus wasn't fit when he joined the PGA Tour. Never mind weighty comparisons, Woods wanted to make sure that everyone recognized the gravity of the Nicklaus run. Was it the end of the Nicklaus era?

Woods and Davis Love III looked at each other as they heard a Nicklaus gallery roar ahead. No words were necessary.

It was a subtle reminder to the new order on the PGA Tour—a sage lesson that the old order is not going to fade into the azaleas. Nicklaus, Crenshaw, Kite, and Watson are not going to turn and say it's your turn. As Nicklaus plays each of the four majors in the year 2000, he's going to claw and grind like the Golden Bear in his prime.

In 1963, when he won his first green jacket, he collected $20,000. Mickleson, Duval, Leonard, and Woods were not yet born. And now, with endorsement deals that stagger the mind, the "kids" on the PGA Tour spill that much on a weekend. Can they understand the escalation of the purses? Or is money creating a blind side to their game?

The young players on the PGA Tour should nod to the players before them. The green fairways were not always so green. Credit for the maturation of the game is due the generation that stamped an indelible impression on the mainstream. The 1990s were as much about the older generation on the PGA Tour as about the kids. Hale Irwin slapping high fives with the gallery at the U.S. Open at Medinah. Ben Crenshaw winning another little green jacket in a spiritual way for the guy who wrote The Little Red Book. Even Mark O'Meara's major run in 1998 was a sign. And the sign of the times reads: *"The game of integrity needs to be nurtured; don't take it for granted."*

In 1998 at Augusta, the response to Nicklaus was inspiring as the fans urged the Golden Bear to make one more patented charge. It was his 40th Masters tournament, and he closed with a final-round 68 on Sunday to finish tied for sixth. His Sunday playing partner, Ernie Els, was captivated by the drama. "I'm 30 years younger, and he beat me by four strokes," said Els.

In 1986, Nicklaus closed with a 65 to edge Greg Norman and Tom Kite by a single stroke. His work at Augusta alone has spanned more than three decades.

Nicklaus has anointed Woods as a guy who will win more green jackets than he has in his closet. He has said Mickleson's finesse around the greens is unparalleled. He has talked one-on-one with Duval, who joined the PGA Tour as a blond, pudgy college phenom, reminiscent of himself. He knows that Justin Leonard has the mind and game of a champion. When Leonard won the U.S. Amateur, it was in Nicklaus' backyard at Muirfield.

Woods grew up with a list of Nicklaus titles next to his bed. Ernie Els has called him his hero on more than one occasion. Lee Westwood was 13 years old when he watched the 1986 Masters. It so inspired the youngster in Worksop, England, that he took up the game.

Nicklaus defined the honor of the game in the way he carried himself. Gary Player, Arnold Palmer, Johnny Miller, and others all created a human element to the game; however, the determination, the graciousness, and the numbers all point to Nicklaus.

Some records will not fall early in the next millennium. Nicklaus claimed 70 PGA Tour wins, including 20 majors. He won at least one tournament each year for a record 17 years (1962 to 1978). Those marks may never be matched. He played on six Ryder Cup teams and captained two teams. He had a total of 286 top 10 finishes on the PGA Tour. The foursome of Leonard, Duval, Woods, and Mickelson has won close to 40 PGA Tour events and three majors combined. But if the U.S. Amateur is considered a major, suddenly, this foursome owns the rights to eight majors.

As the young players slowly emerge on the leader boards, will they remember their forefathers? Leonard hardly does an interview without discussing the history of the game. Woods and Mickelson often refer to Mr. Nelson, Mr. Palmer, and Mr. Nicklaus, acknowledging their contributions to the game and the genuine spirit with which they competed. Woods likens his final-round red apparel to the same aura, that Gary Player's black outfits represented. The reverence exists and the salutation begins with sir. Woods said, "I wasn't able to see Mr. Nelson play. I wasn't able to see how great he really was. It was before my time. But I grew up watching Jack." He means Mr. Nicklaus.

It is Nicklaus who admitted, "Arnold Palmer brought the game out of the dark ages."

At the 1999 Memorial Tournament, there was sense that Jack extended his hand to Tiger. Jack's time in the sun had been surpassed by a "different" game. "I think everybody has a different way of playing the game. I've never seen this way of playing before. I don't mean that from a funny standpoint," said Nicklaus.

Without pointing fingers, Nicklaus indicated that the 20-something players might be in one class and Tiger Woods in another. "I don't know if anybody can play the way he plays. He has the ability to do things that nobody else can do," added Nicklaus. Close your eyes and remember the early descriptions of Nicklaus, and the tone and statements are uncanny.

Paired with Ben Hogan at Cherry Hills in 1960, Nicklaus, a 20-year-old amateur, failed to make a run as Palmer charged ahead to win by two strokes. "I'm sure I walked away copying his (Hogan's) swing the next couple of months. I always did that. I remember playing with Sam (Snead). That's what kids do." Seven years later, at the 1967 U.S. Open at Baltusrol, Nicklaus, now

27, was emerging on the scene to beat Palmer and a little-known Texan named Lee Trevino.

Woods didn't see firsthand how Nicklaus dominated fields and dissected courses, but the legend lives on. "He's the greatest ever. There's nobody else who has the records that he has. I saw where he had 70 top 10s in the majors. I was thinking, well, that's a major, only four a year," Woods said. "And he was able to do that for a very long period of time." Duval, always the stoic, recognizes that Nicklaus' numbers may be a thing of the past.

He said, "I just don't know how long I'm going to play. They say your late '20s, 29 up to 36 is when everybody hits their prime. Boy, I sure hope so." Duval has a relaxed attitude about the future. "I think in today's game, with the players who are playing, the competition, and you play a career of 15 years, whatever it may be, and you leave the game with 20 wins. Something like that, you've had a hell of a run."

Duval is a perfect role model in persistence, even though the kid who was called "pudgy like Nicklaus" is more impressed by a Nicklaus trademark. "He was pretty infamous about letting everybody beat themselves. That is the approach I try to take, because I realize and know that as we're playing, people are going to make mistakes. I just keep plugging along like Nicklaus," said Duval.

Nicklaus further reflects on the perception of players like Duval and Woods. "I'm sure a lot of kids turn around and look at this old man, and say, 'We're getting experience playing with him.' But those kids get in the fairway. I don't even get in the fairway anymore." It is hard for Leonard, Duval, Woods, and Mickelson to compare their games to Nicklaus, because when Nicklaus was in his prime, Philip, Justin, David, and Tiger were not even competitive junior players. Mark O'Meara said, "I think Jack Nicklaus is by far the greatest player who's ever played the game of golf. And I know when Jack was dominating, he hit the ball much longer than anyone else, but I'm not so sure he hit it as far as Tiger hits it." Ask O'Meara about the short game, and he points to the collective kids on Tour.

"I think David Duval has a wonderful short game. I think Tiger is a good chipper of the ball. We all know Phil Mickelson is very creative around the greens. I think Justin Leonard has a great short game. These guys have tremendous short games. And I think that's an aspect you have to have."

As everyone who has studied Nicklaus knows, the game is larger than 14 clubs, a caddie and 18 holes. The mental game is an internal war for each player; the one who avoids turmoil usually ends up holding the trophy. At Pinehurst, Nicklaus talked about of this test of wills. "I love listening to players gripe. 'The rough is too high'; check him off. 'The greens are too fast; check him off.' Guys complain themselves right out of this championship."

Hogan vs. Snead, Palmer vs. Nicklaus, Nicklaus vs. Watson. In a sport epitomized as an individual confrontation with nature, why has the prospect of a man vs. man battle continued to stand at the core? Has it carried over from tennis, where the visage of both athletes is as evident as it is in golf. The emotions are plain and apparent. Both Duval and Woods have talked about the media's portrayal of the western-like anticipatory tournament jousting between the two players.

"I think they both feel they're not playing against each other; they're trying to figure out how to win a major championship. And I just think time needs to take care of that," said Nicklaus. This is wisdom from the king addressed to the heirs apparent of the throne, but don't look for Nicklaus to look on the other fairway. "Are rivalries good for the game? Yeah, I think they're fun for the game," he said. The made for television, prime-time event called the Showdown at Sherwood was a forced union that both

Woods and Duval agreed would bring the game to a larger audience.

"A one-day, 18-hole match, that alone does not make a rivalry," said Duval. He also added, "I think Tiger is a player, one of several players, who will always be motivating to other players, solely because you're going to have to improve and get better. But, at the same time, I'm a firm believer that if you need motivation from outside sources, you're not going to go very far."

Both players are represented by the International Management Group (IMG), the same group headed by Mark McCormack that recognized the marketing savvy of Palmer. Woods represents the same kind of charisma, but it's now a high-tech playing field. McCormack recently commented that "Palmer was to Thomas Edison what "Woods is to Bill Gates." Nicklaus' light is flickering, but the kids on tour want to carry the light. Woods said, "He (Nicklaus) set the bar very high. Watching him still hit range balls. He still has perfect traj. I'm thinking, wow, if I'm as old as he is, I'd like to be able just to walk."

Mr. Nicklaus will continue to have an indirect impression on the courses the millennium kids play. His early design work with both Pete Dye (Harbour Town) and Desmond Muirhead (Muirfield) shows a versatility of design and a spirit to challenge both today's and tomorrow's players. The MCI Classic and the Memorial Tournaments are anchor events on the PGA Tour.

Before the Memorial Championship, Tiger Woods said, "One reason I come here is the person who represents the event. Mr. Nicklaus." To Tiger, Phil, Justin, David, Ernie, Sergio, and the rest of the young players on tour, Mr. Nicklaus is not a phantom. He represents the progression of a game. But the emergence of the field of young competitors breeds new life in some of the veteran players like Mark O'Meara. "I feel like Tiger and young players like David Duval and Justin Leonard are the future in the game. But that's not to say they can't be beaten."

O'Meara admits that playing with Woods may have been the single most important factor that elevated his game in 1998 to capture two majors. O'Meara insists that the kids, namely Woods, have changed the game in so many ways. Tiger Woods, David Duval, Justin Leonard, and Phil Mickelson are just a few of the names who have motivated and inspired the older generation to step up their games.

It was not so long ago that experience was irreplaceable. This shot requires "experience." To accomplish a good number on this layout, it will take a player with "experience." The "experienced" player will play the shot like this. You've heard Peter Kostis say it, Ken Venturi, Gary McCord, the people with their hand on the microphone and the pulse of the game. But does the PGA Tour need to check the pulse of the young players?

Nicklaus concedes that they have "changed the way everyone approaches the game." In 1999, experience was in second place. It was not a "word" that was muttered when Rich Beem won the Kemper or Glen Day responded at Hilton Head or Brent Geiberger picked up the trophy at the Canon Greater Hartford Open. The number of players competing at a high level has indeed started to erase the word "experience." The younger players will soon be looking behind them to an even younger batch of players with the instincts to compete.

One reason for this is college golf, and another reason is the Nike Tour. Tim Finchem has all the pieces in place. The Nike Tour is the one cornerstone of *experience* for the younger player. The Nike Tour is sending schools of fish to the PGA Tour pond with piranha-like instincts. When Duval (8th on the 1994 money list) and Furyk (26th on the 1993 money list) played the Nike Tour, it was extremely competitive. The likes of Tom Lehman, John Daly, Chris Smith, Stewart Cink and Skip Kendall are making big splashes on the big boys' circuit. Guys like Nicklaus, Trevino, and Floyd did not have the minor league tour to prepare them for the competition. They weren't afforded a proving ground. Check out minor league baseball, hockey, and other sports with feeder programs. There is exceptional talent combusting in the minor leagues, and golf is no exception.

Nicklaus went from the Scarlet course at Ohio State and the 1961 NCAA Championship and climbed aboard the PGA Tour. He did not have the opportunity to test his skills at another level. Duval finished eighth on the 1994 Nike Tour money list to get his card. Leonard, in large part because of his third-place finish at the Anheuser-Busch Golf Classic, gained full exempt status in 1994. Woods seized the opportunity by winning twice in 1996 to launch his career. Mickelson's entry onto the PGA Tour was due to his Northern Telecom win in 1991 as an amateur. Different paths to success. There is not a single cookie-cutter approach to the game at the top level.

Are the kids on tour turning back the clock? The average age of the 1997 major winners was 26.5. In 1987, Woods was launching his junior golf career, Leonard was starting to win junior tournaments, and Els was waiting to get accepted for a couple national junior events on the west coast, like the Optimist World. And in 1987, Larry Mize, Scott Simpson, Nick Faldo, and Larry Nelson were not exactly the collective kids on Tour. Their average age was 37.75. What do the next 10 years hold? Who's to say that a 20-year-old named Sergio Garcia won't rebound from being the low amateur in 1999 to challenge for the green jacket in 2000? Can Tiger Woods, at 24 be any better than he was at 21?

Tom Watson played in his first senior event in 1999. Hale Irwin and Ray Floyd have made the jump. Is the progression to the younger player an alternative or just plain fate? Brad Faxon pointed out, "Like in any sport, the players are getting younger. One concern I have for the junior player is burnout." Will the aggressive play of Woods from the tee be around in 10 years? Will the game allow a player like Tiger Woods to retire when he's

35? As we say goodbye to Wayne Gretzky, Michael Jordan, Barry Sanders, and John Elway, long, successful careers a thing of the past? Look at the years Nicklaus (17) and Palmer (15) spent in the top 10 on the money list. Tom Watson led the money list for four years (1977 to 1980). Can we again expect to see this kind of dominance?

It took Tiger Woods just nine events to win $1 million, and 16 events to win $2 million on the PGA Tour. Players like Johnny Miller and Lee Trevino won a little more than that in their whole careers on tour.

As Nicklaus will remind each player, the game of golf is more about elevating the game. Creating a spirit behind the championships is more important than endorsing a check. Woods, Mickleson, Duval, and Leonard are the youngest four American players ever to win their first million on the PGA Tour, but each has the will to make more than a ball mark's impression on the leader boards at majors. Nicklaus developed a passion for conquering the golf course and overtaking humanity in the process. Duval and Woods have shown the hunger. Leonard and Mickelson have shown that they know how to compete.

Tom Watson is a great example of a golfer who was able to kiss five claret jugs, don two green jackets and win a glorious U.S. Open at Pebble Beach. He had a run of four years where he took what ability he had and turned it up a notch in the majors.

At the 2023 Masters, will Tiger Woods, at the age of 48 sit down in Butler Cabin and put his arms through the sleeves of his eighth green jacket? The younger players of today know the importance of nutrition, fitness, the benefit of playing in fewer events. What has happened to the game is that the business side of the sport has grown so fast that the sport itself has partly begun to play second fiddle to economics. What the young players are going to have to guard against is not Barry Burns or out-of-bounds markers, but what Brad Faxon calls "burn-out." Can these guys take a timeout for a New York minute and breathe the fresh blossoms of the azaleas at Amen Corner? Can they smile at the cruel wind at St. Andrew's?

The kids of today at junior golf tournaments do not really understand the Nicklaus era. Tiger Woods is their role model. Johnny Miller said, "I've never seen it where kids think he's (Woods) a kid. So it's like he's one of them. They want to know what he wears and how he carries himself and how hard he swings. The junior golfers want to know why Tiger hits it so far." Miller was around when Ben Crenshaw came on tour, and he called it an "excitement," but Miller admits the game has changed, and the mainstream of today's junior players have a firm hold on the popularity of the game. And like a 3-wood over a lake to a green guarded by bunkers, they are going to grip it tight.

Since the AJGA was formed, the decorum and integrity of the games was constantly a board of directors agenda item. How are the kids acting at tournaments? What is the level of sportsmanship? Are the crimes in society trickling down into youth sports? In a game that tests character by the second, the junior players either follow the rules or they're gone. An AJGA code of conduct is strictly enforced at AJGA tournaments. Miller admitted that junior golf has stood the test of teenage delinquency.

"I go to collegiate events, I go to amateur events, and I go to junior events. There will always be some kids who come in with no clue, but the core group is as well behaved and together as it's ever been in history. We run tournaments (the Johnny Miller Junior) and we don't even have an incident. Nowadays, if you throw a club, you're out of there."

Miller reminds junior golfers at his tournament that there was a time when showing more emotion was accepted on the course. "There was a Connors, McEnroe, and Nastasie time. I remember when I was a 10-year-old, watching Arnold Palmer play. At least three times he buried his club down past the hosel.

I watched it, saying, 'I guess that's what you do when you miss an iron, huh, Dad?' My dad just said, 'No, you don't need to do that.'"

Pete Ripa was roaming the course at a recent AJGA event when he heard the roar of a single junior player from an adjacent green. The word Ripa heard was the one players normally hear when a putt lips out or just misses the edge. In his tournament cart, Ripa sped to find the unsuspecting player at the next tee. Ripa stopped his cart and asked, "O K, who missed the putt?" He surveyed the threesome on the tee box with a jury's intent. The player unable to make eye contact was easily identifiable. Ripa simply said, "Add a stroke at the end of your round. I'll see you at the clubhouse." The AJGA has instituted a code of conduct on and off the course at it's events, and it has helped maintain the balance of respect that the game should be afforded. Respect and a foundation of the rules of golf are so important to the growing integrity of the game.

Phil Mickelson's father echoes the importance of the decorum. "There is a certain integrity and character that goes with the game of golf when it is played right. If you can include that in your daily living and your family, you're much better for it," he said.

In an unforgiving game, even the young players need a common ground of stability to stand the tide. Johnny Miller is a good example of a player who went on a run in the early 1970s before turning a lot of attention to his family. He said, "As soon as you establish that being a father is a bigger deal than golfing, it's very tough to keep golf as a priority because it softens you. That's what happened to me. I got softened by my family, which is good. I'm happy about that. So a lot will depend on what happens with marriage and kids and all that stuff."

It is obvious that Mickelson approached fatherhood at the U.S. Open. Woods and Leonard might be the farthest twosome from starting a family. But Duval and his longtime girlfriend, Julie MacArthur, a pharmacist from Atlanta, might be getting close to a prescription for marriage. As Miller found out, family life affected him in a positive way, but as he said, "It is very difficult to stay hungry when the baby comes out. It is a heck of a lot more important than your golf game."

Miller is just one example of how family affects a player's life on the PGA Tour. And with the importance of the word *family* to Mickelson, there is a sense that the foundation of his own family might be the impetus for him to escalate his career. Nicklaus is a great example of how he coupled his family life with golf. He will continue to be an ambassador of the game he helped build. He will continue to counsel many of the star young players in the game.

As the Golden Bear tracks show up at the majors in 2000, it will be interesting to see which of the young cubs on the PGA Tour follow closely behind.

The 18th hole at Valhalla Golf Club in Eastwood, Kentucky, is a 536-yard par 5. Players in the 2000 PGA will play across Floyds Fork to a mounded fairway. Then, they will have a decision to play a conservative shot to the left, where there is a less-than-advantageous entry to the green. Or they can play to the right of the large bunker dividing the fairway. This route is a little more risky, but allows for a better approach to the multi-tiered green. Valhalla was designed by Nicklaus. He has said it will likely be the last major in which he competes. The last hole is a symbol of the direction of the young players on the PGA Tour. When Nicklaus holes out on 18 at Valhalla, there will be a hollowed absence. It will be a challenge for the kids of the PGA Tour. What fork in the fairway will the next generation of the PGA Tour take once he's gone?

Chapter 6

THE CADDYSHACK
GENERATION

The crowd has grown deadly silent. Four golfers named Justin Leonard, Tiger Woods, Phil Mickelson, and David Duval are all Cinderella stories from outta nowhere. Even though Woods wasn't a former greenskeeper, he can hit a 2-iron about 455 yards. We know Leonard earned a scholarship to play for Jimmy Clayton at Texas, so he didn't have to work in the lumberyard like Danny. And before Mickelson met his wife, Amy, he probably saw a few monkey women like Mrs. Crane in the gallery. But whatever you do, make sure you never ask Duval if he ever caddied for the Dalai Lama, because before any of these players turned eleven, Director Harold Ramis assembled a pretty good foursome himself. It included Ty Webb (Chevy Chase), Judge Smails (Ted Knight), Carl Spackler (Bill Murray) and Al Czervik (Rodney Dangerfield).

Caddyshack, released in 1980, took the sport of golf and funneled the game like a burrowing gopher from the snobs of the mythic Bushwood Country Club, through the lumberyard, to the mainstream. It made the sport cool. It took the serious side of the sport and slam-dunked it like a Baby Ruth bar in Rae's Creek. All of a sudden, the game took on a humorous side that was so intangible that the golfing world will never recover. Correct me if I'm wrong, but the movie *Caddyshack* took America's grip on the sport and eased the tension. The movie lit the fuse like Carl Spackler's plastic explosives, and it slowly ignited and combusted into laughter on tee boxes and putting greens.

Caddyshack vernacular became a common ground of communication for every kid from Hans Albertsson in Manchester, Vermont, to Sal Spallone in Vero Beach, Florida, to Bob May in LaHabra, California. Some of the people yukking it up were the nation's college golf coaches. Puggy Blackmon said, "It is kind of like a Grateful Dead thing. It's really turned into a cult-like following. From David Duval to the freshmen on my team, everyone who has ever played for me knows that movie."

Blackmon's golf camp counselors can do a running skit of several scenes from the movie with a simple prompt, for example, "It's in the hole." Coach Jim Brown at Ohio State said, "All my guys have watched that movie so many times, they keep repeating every line." *Tin Cup* and *Happy Gilmore* are like Brady Bunch reruns compared to the movie that Blackmon called the *"Gone with the Wind* of golf."

The new millennium marks the movie's 20th anniversary. Bob Wood, president of Nike Golf, ponders the impact of the movie and then goes on a five-minute conservation between Danny and Judge Smails. He says, "The first time I watched it, I was on my back, laughing hysterically. It was on cable and I watched it three times in a 24-four hour period."

Can you say that any other single event, tournament, golf club or ball that has so shaped the personae the game? Arnold Palmer had charisma, and Nicklaus had the skills and mental capacity to overcome a golf course. But no entertainment medium has ever been so impactive in its influence on a sport by virtue of a single film?

Brad Faxon said, "Everybody loves it on tour. You don't have to be a golfer to like the movie. It is a lot like *Austin Powers*. It wasn't a huge box office, but it has become a rental smash." *Austin Powers* shagged movie fanatics, but the longevity of a script written by Brian Doyle Murray and Douglas Kenney has now spanned generations.

"The thing I like about the movie is that 60-year-olds can relate, and so can Tiger Woods and kids even younger," said Wood. Even non-golfers appreciate the universal humor. They realize that they may not have a chance to score in the 70s, but come their deathbed, they will have a real chance of receiving a most precious gift—total consciousness—and that's not all bad.

It's interesting that *Caddyshack* made the game a melting pot of interests at a time when the sport was divided. There was a brick wall between the country-club set and the municipal course weekend warriors. *Caddyshack* took the humbling game past the threshold of pressure and into a universal acceptance for its oddities. It shared a respect for the finite abilities of the characters portrayed: a young kid searching for a caddie scholarship, a judge searching for the skill, the most skilled player at Bushwood seeking a higher power. Nearly everyone found compassion for the dreaded lowest man on the food chain, even below the lowly gopher—the laboring greenskeeper. Carl Spackler was not out to kill "gophers," he somehow proved that "golfers" are not the only ones important to the game.

In the late 80s each of the 20-something players at one time stood on a green or a tee and heard words like "Thousand bucks says you'll slice this one," or "Miss it, Noonan." The sport was turning toward the masses as a sport for the ages, and *Caddyshack* was a small B movie that made a big impact in that direction. The kids in junior golf used the *Caddyshack* vernacular to banter and elevate gamesmanship. With the timing of *Caddyshack* and the development of a national junior circuit, suddenly there was an aspect to the game that was more than shooting a low score. The game was not just for adults, it was also for kids.

Has the impact of *Caddyshack* faded? Just last year the American Junior Golf Association mixed in *Caddyshack* trivia with its rules sessions before tournaments. Pete Ripa, associate executive director, said, "I did not think these kids would be able to get any of the answers of the questions."

One of the first trivia challenges was "Recite Judge Smails' speech when he christened his yacht." The initial murmur was contagious in the room, which was packed with over 150 junior players. A young man stood up and boldly proclaimed, *"It's easy to grin/ When your ship comes in/ And you've got the stock market beat./ But the man worthwhile/ Is the man who can smile/ When his shorts are too tight in the seat."* The room erupted. Bravo! Next question.

Certain events in the movie have created even more pressure to the millennium sport of millimeters. The game of golf is not void of vices. It was Judge Smails who once said, "Gambling is illegal at Bushwood, and I never slice." Can anyone blame David Duval and Clark Burroughs for tossing a few Andrew Jacksons in the cart to reach a competitive climate on Tuesdays at Nike Tour events?

Even Gary McCord, as he walked alongside Phil Mickelson, has offered a friendly $20 wager for the left-hander to make a putt. At one time, even the AJGA staff would assemble a rotisserie format for the week's tournaments. Longtime AJGA staffer Pete Ripa was among the tournament staff members at the 1987 Meridian Classic in Denver helping to compile a rotisserie team. In the second round, Ripa pondered his selection. After a moment of silence, he said, "I'm taking Not-a-big-guy" (at least that's what he said). The other AJGA staffers checked their tournament pairings sheets to look for Ripa's pick. After everyone participating exhausted his pairings sheet, Ripa then pointed out that he wanted a kid from New Mexico named Notah Begay. This was long before Begay putted from both sides of the ball, went to Stanford and shot 59. While Justin Leonard was missing his tee time at Meridian, Begay was winning the title in the boys' 11-14 age group and earning Ripa low scores for his rotisserie team.

As tournament purses escalate, and as the game's technology jibes with the velocity of club-head speed, can something as simple as a fun-loving movie impact the game of golf in the next millennium?

Consider the next generation of the PGA Tour as the *Caddyshack* Generation. They're playing the game because it's cool. They're playing the game because it's challenging—they're just "being the ball".

THE WIND AND THE FURYK

It was not an Elvis sighting, but to 17- and 18-year-old college golf wannabes, the mere mention of Mike Holder's name was enough to send a quart of adrenaline through the mega-hormoned bodies of prospective student-athletes. Holder's Oklahoma State men's golf program had a reputation as the best golf team in America. His Cowboys had won the 1987 national championship a month earlier, and he had now turned his attention to his sport's lifeblood, recruiting.

Holder was checking out the scoreboard at Meadowbrook Country Club, the site of the Oklahoma Junior Classic, as the leader groups in the boy's 15-18 age group traversed the front nine. Back on the course, Kevin Wentworth, a left-hander, took out a driver and sent his tee shot down the middle of the 7th fairway. His playing partner, Greg Gill, did the same. Wentworth and Gill were paired with Jim Furyk, the kid with the funky swing from Manheim, Pennsylvania. Wentworth and Gill had the clean-cut looks and the silky swings, certain targets for Mike Holder's program. Another clean-cut kid with a smooth swing, Brian Watts, led the Cowboy team to the national championship that year.

With Wentworth and Gill down the middle in good shape, Furyk teed up his ball to the far right of the tee box. His course management taught him that his left-to-right shot needed a margin for error, even if it meant a few extra steps on the tee box. Furyk cocked the club up to the top of his backswing and then lowered the shaft of the driver into position to launch his tee shot. Just as his club-head made contact with the ball, a loud explosion from the tee box surprised the players. The other players could not find the flight of Furyk's golf ball. Instead, they looked for what triggered the sound. The plastic, round tee marker had received the impact of Furyk's shot. The ball had careened off the tee marker and popped up in the air about 75 yards from the tee box. Furyk, embarrassed by his misguided tee ball, tugged his bag on his shoulder and lumbered down the fairway.

Holder did not witness the exploding tee ball, but talk of what caused the sound quickly made its way back to the clubhouse. Holder was unabashed in his reaction. "I've never seen that happen," said the national championship coach, as he began his search for more talent for his squad.

Furyk tied for second at the Oklahoma Junior Classic, two shots off the winning pace set by Brad McCollum. Two weeks later, at the Ben Hogan Boys' Junior played at Gleneagles Country Club (Queens Course), Furyk shot one better (71-73-70) than he had in Oklahoma, and he beat Rob McKelvey on the first sudden-death hole to win his first national junior championship.

Furyk had more hair in 1987, but the same swing—a swing his father, Mike, helped him refine growing up in eastern Pennsylvania. It was Furyk's physical development that possibly tilted the scale in his favor during junior golf.

"Furyk was more mature physically. In fact, if you took a comparison of his body frame as a 17-year-old and his body frame now, there is not much difference," said AJGA executive director Stephen Hamblin.

Furyk was a classic top 10 finisher in junior golf. His consistency enabled him to be named to the 1987 AJGA All-America first team. Furyk manufactured his swing and his parents' finances to gain a golf scholarship to the University of Arizona. Head coach Rick LaRose was building a program that eventually won the 1992 national championship, in Furyk's senior year.

Furyk graduated from the University of Arizona to the Nike Tour. In 1993, on the Nike Tour, he ground out 25 events and finished 26th on the money list, but he saved his best play for the 1993 Q-school. An Arizona teammate, Harry Rudolph, said, "Once he got his ball striking down, he was able to put the mental side to work. He was such a phenomenal saver. Once he put it all together, it was just a matter of time. He always putted like a madman."

It was exactly one decade removed from his best junior summer that the wind in Furyk's swing caught flames. When Furyk shot a Wednesday pro-am 63 at the Byron Nelson Classic, something in his quirky swing had clicked. He had the confidence to attack both the Cottonwood Valley and the TPC at Las Colinas. He picked up Thursday where he left off with an opening-round 63 to lead the field. This would be the low round of the year for Furyk. He was one stroke ahead of Tiger Woods. Thursday's play was aided by a storm that rolled through Dallas. Furyk finished the tournament 67-67-71 and tied for fifth.

His summer run went something like this: Tied for fifth at the Byron Nelson; eighth place at the Mastercard Colonial; tied for second at the Memorial; tied for fifth at the U.S. Open; tied for third at the Buick Classic; tied for fourth at the British Open; tied for seventh at the Sprint International; tied for sixth at the PGA Championship. Two top 10 majors, six other top 10 and the fury was all about money. He garnered $1,619,480 in 1997 to finish fourth on the money list. Only Tiger Woods, Davis Love III, and David Duval's closing run finished ahead of Mr.

Consistency. Justin Leonard claimed two wins (Kemper and the British Open) over the same stretch, but not as much money.

Furyk had arrived on the PGA Tour. The tour statistics reflected his turnaround—fifth in driving accuracy, sixth in putting and seventh in scoring average. A classic top 10 finisher in junior golf and now a lot of top 10 statistical rankings for the guy with a lot of top 10 finishes.

Furyk continues to hang around the money on the PGA Tour. In 1998, he tied Duval with the most (12) top 10 finishes and netted more than $2 million on the PGA Tour. This put him right behind Duval and Woods in third place on the money list. He joined with Duval to win the Fred Meyer Challenge and won the 1998 Las Vegas Invitational for his third win on Tour.

Furyk may not have a picturesque swing, but his results in majors do not lie. In the last three British Opens, he has done no worse than a tie for 6th (1999). At Carnoustie, he finished with a closing-round 70, just five strokes out of the playoff. And at the 1996 and 1997 U.S Opens, he tied for fifth.

Furyk has won as much money and had more consistent finishes than a lot of the younger players on the PGA Tour, and he is on the verge of breaking through at a major championship. He was in position at Medinah before he drifted down the leader board.

However, his 1998-99 seasons earned him a return to the Ryder Cup at Brookline. Whether he's shattering tee markers or breaking through to a major championship, the wind behind Furyk's swing will carry him as a player to watch in the new millennium.

Y2K KIDS

The new generation of the PGA Tour will take a high-tech game into the next millennium. Cell phones, laptop computers, titanium shafts, big metal-headed drivers, supercharged golf balls, and muscles all mark the new direction of the sport, and not just on the PGA Tour.

As the new millennium of the PGA Tour dawns, the game's most brutal battle will be the one waged off the course and away from the clubhouse. Forget Duval versus Woods and the Ryder Cup financial breakdown. Take a step back and taste the $1.50 sandwich at Augusta National. What effect has the science of technology had on the game of tradition? Or, maybe, what effect has the business of golf had on tradition.com.

The most significant change over the past 50 years might be golf's playing field—the courses, those asymmetrical battle-fields where the young turks and the wily veterans send a dimpled sphere to lengthening 7,000 yards-plus courses, stopping just 18 times below the surface of the earth. Part of the Y2K kids' plan includes becoming more and more compatible at places like Augusta, Pebble Beach, the Old Course and Valhalla in 2000. And the sport has come to be defined by words like "manicured" and "groomed." Champion acceptance speeches with a tip-of-the-big-dollar-endorsed cap to the greens' staff is like signing the scorecard. It is never more evident than at the majors.

The "U.S. Open rough," the "porcelain greens at Augusta" and the "convex greens at Pinehurst" have punctuated the tournaments and elevated the players who have conquered the course. Overcoming the courses, nature's obstacles, and the devilish PGA Tour and USGA Rules Committee tests, such as pin placements and shaved greens, is more important than any media-created rivalry. Not far behind major agronomy vernacular is second-tier gallery chatter regarding the texture of sand in bunkers, the contour of fairways and the maturation of once-sibling trees.

On the eve of the millennium, changes to Augusta National, such as pushing tee boxes back and elongating certain holes, is a hint of what's to come. But before the conversation doglegs to playability, how do the conditions dictate the competition? How did these green venues come to pass?

Can the game's roots in America be traced to designers like Donald Ross? Nobody fashioned green quite like the Scotsman Ross during the early part of the 20th century. From his start at Pinehurst, Ross was mentored early on by old Tom Morris, and he used that knowledge to literally shape America's playing fields. He also shaped every player's approach to the game like a driving- range balata.

What happens after Ross, Tom Fazio, Albert Warren, Tillinghast, Pete Dye, and Jack Nicklaus stamp their design in the soil and the seed is sown? The answer is really a subtle reminder in course etiquette. It's easy to recognize architecture and design and applaud those who painted the canvas, but what about the people who preserved and nurtured the terrain? It's an age-old question: nature or nurture? Ask Sam Snead and Kathy Whitworth about the greatest technological advancement in the game and the answer is simple—"turf equipment." Strike up a conversation with the venerable Byron Nelson and ask him about the evolution of the game: his oratory on agronomy takes off like a sculled 8-iron. It puts a wry smile on his face and dimples in his cheeks. The knowledge of grass and the improvement of turf equipment have advanced tremendously in the past century. Watch Golf Channel replays of the Masters Tournament in the 1960s, and it is very evident. Augusta National, by today's standards, looked like a glorified municipal track.

The science of agronom,y through applications like verticutting and aeration, have created a renaissance in America's courses from tee to green. It is not so evident to the 20-something players on the PGA Tour, but you take the question to the Nicklaus, Palmer, and Crenshaw set, and the response is alarming. The veteran throwback competitors on the PGA Tour have turned to nature's vast playground to continue their careers. Jack, Arnie, and Ben once shaped the golf ball with precision, and now they're shaping the game as course designers by taking navigable barren land and sculpting it into a brown, contoured underbelly. Then comes the embryonic stage when the seed initializes the end of the pregnancy and the beginning of the maturation.

Nicklaus, Palmer and Crenshaw have saddled their careers away from the game in the mode of Ross. They have revamped the game from making competitive moves on the leader board to getting competitive about moving dirt. They pioneer their new trade for what Crenshaw called, "the potential for great golf." The game stops every week at well-groomed arenas. It starts with bulldozers and ends with stimpmeters. It wasn't always that way. Long before Bill Murray's character, Carl Spackler, in *Caddyshack,* there were guys who only knew how to cut grass. Now, there are greens superintendents making more than some of the PGA our's card-toting members. The PGA Tour has a staff of five agronomists, headed by Jon Scott. But the PGA Tour did not always keep a finger on the pulse of nature—more specifically, agronomy.

In the 1920s, the U.S. Department of Agriculture started getting serious about researching turf management. It set up turf plots close to the Pentagon and developed tests to determine the best conditions for different seeds and their adaptability to various conditions. Major universities soon developed an interest in testing soils. The USGA also got involved, and before long, the science of agronomy was knee deep in its own research, which eventually found its way to the game of golf.

Scott remembers witnessing the development of the research side of his business: "Initially, there was not a whole lot of money allocated to do research, but we have come a long way just in terms of testing since then." Scott, a 1972 graduate of Michigan State University, worked with Jack Nicklaus' agronomy staff for nine years before joining the PGA Tour three years ago. He spent a year at the Grand Traverse Resort (a Nicklaus design) doing a grow-in for the Bear course. He also spent time at another Nicklaus layout, Valhalla (the site of the 2000 PGA Championship) in Louisville, where he helped salvage what he terms "a bad grow-in." Scott has seen the fairways become greener and it is evident to him that the sport "is on the cutting edge of turf science technology."

Scott points to the advent of certain turf maintenance devices that have, in his eyes, "revolutionized" the game. A five-plex fairway mower, that is able to efficiently mow grass to a millimeter's height, was once a luxury and has now become a necessity. In golfing circles, the lightweight five-plex and its predecessor, the tri-plex have become more important to turf barns than the mini van has for middle America.

Scott said, "It started with the triplex mower in the 1970s, because that was the only alternative to the heavier, gang-type mowers we used to use on fairways." The only disadvantage to using the triplex was efficiency. Mowing par 4s and 5s with the triplex took a long time. The five-plex eliminated the efficiency problem and helped increase the condition of the fairways by increasing the blade reels.

"Once you take the weight stress off the fairways, the grass gets healthier. The precision of the cuts is better because there are more blades on the reels, so you get a higher frequency of hit. It gives you overall more density in the grass, which creates the velvety look of so many of the PGA Tour fairways of today," said Scott. The turf maintenance staff, still prefers the tri-plex mower for its fairways. Nicklaus is a throwback competitor in more than one arena of the game.

The other chief improvement has been in the area of irrigation. Golf courses are taking advantage of the advances in irrigation technology to grow grass and "keep it green." Watering systems, synchronized by timers, syringe greens regularly to accommodate dry seasons and protect the playing field. This upkeep also separates America's courses from the distinct terrain of European courses.

Scott said, "Many of the British course, have irrigation systems, but there is just a difference in philosophy. Americans like green. And where the game evolved over there with little or no irrigation, brown is what is considered tournament quality."

Most of America's courses are parkland courses versus the wind-swept links-style courses in Europe. As Scott said, "Golf evolved in the United Kingdom along the coastline, and it gave them a mind-set of what a golf course should look like."

Scott experiments with different playing conditions and different grass types each week on the PGA Tour. His staff works with each PGA Tour stop at least a year in advance so that they can accommodate every aspect of greens maintenance when the tournament week approaches for "two weeks of high stress." Scott's not talking about the stress on the staff as much as he's talking about the stress of the grass, primarily, the stress on the root system and the burden of getting a consistency of pace on every green. Scott's staff works closely with the PGA Tour rules committee and the tournament staffs from week to week to create a fair playground. In the eyes of some players, fair is determined by how far up the leader board they finish on Sunday.

Twenty players who do make the cut each week receive a questionnaire from Scott's staff. We want to produce the conditions they want. "We get immediate feedback from the rules officials, and the players' responses usually back that up," said Scott.

In 1980, Scott Simpson won his first PGA Tour event at Butler National. The greens were brown because they were ravaged by turf disease. Twenty years later, and the words "*turf disease*" might hamper the Mickelson backyard, but not the tournament courses on the PGA Tour. Poa annua might be the newest Telletubbie, but it's not a problem on greens on the PGA Tour. "We are way ahead of the curve when it comes to turf-disease prevention," said Scott. But, he adds, "We have such an arsenal of research that we will not have another Butler, where it wiped out their greens."

One specific disease called Gray Leaf Spot has damaged courses in the Northeast. A couple of current PGA Senior Tour and Nike Tour events currently fight the disease, which, Scott says, "If it spreads, it can wipe out a fairway of turf in just a couple of days."

Scott insists that mower technology, irrigation, and the controlling of turf disease has prepared the game for the new millennium. But he knows that the stimpmeter (the device that calculates the speed of the greens) is one of the most-talked-about readings among players, the rules committee, and the agronomy staff—at least on Tuesday and Wednesday.

"We have to watch ourselves," said Scott. Like what happened with the 18th hole at the Olympic Club in the 1998 U.S.

Open. A shaved green, a bad pin placement, and the PGA Tour players start asking to add windmills and alligators. Because of turf conditions and the catch-all word "playability," Scott works to have greens running from 9 to 11 1/2 on the stimpmeter.

From the canvas to the brush. High-tech conversation on compatibility might start with the courses, but before long, the discussion zeros in on the smallest piece of equipment—the supercharged golf ball. Golf ball wars have replaced pizza as the leading America retail frenzy. Callaway and Nike have entered the golf ball fray being waged at the top between dominant players like Titleist and Maxfli.

It was 100 years ago (1900) when Coburn Haskell invented the first rubber thread-wound golf ball surrounded by a rubber core. The realization of his idea was met with some obstacles, like how to wind and mass produce thousands of balls. Around 1905, William Taylor took Haskell's inner core and introduced the concave dimples to the exterior, that provided superior aerodynamics. A year later, A.G. Spalding ran ads calling his golf balls "The longest and truest flyers." Six dollars a dozen would get the player Spalding's "click" (for the sound they made when the hit the face of the club) balls with "dots." Players would often have to paint the balls once they played a couple of rounds because they would become dark. Despite the number of manufacturers that have entered the product category, golf balls have really not changed much. More than 90 percent of the players on the PGA Tour play a wound ball today.

Has technology gone too far? Square grooves in the '80s and titanium shafts and big metal drivers in the '90s have made some historic golf course layouts obsolete for the proven player. The four words, "I've bought a game" echo from pro shops throughout the land. Justin Leonard recently described his switch to a metal driver by saying, "What's permanent in this game? Who knows what will happen?" Addressing the World Scientific

Congress of Golf, Titleist CEO Wally Uihlein said, "The issue is the balance between the forces of tradition and technology and the degree to which these forces remain in balance as we prepare the game, and the game prepares for us, for the next millennium."

The game must somehow absorb the shock of technology. Founded in 1996, the World Scientific Congress of Golf was organized by the Royal & Ancient Golf Club, the USGA, and the University of St. Andrew to promote and disseminate golf-related research. Uihlein and the World Scientific Congress of Golf members' rhetoric revolves around the "future of golf's landscape."

Although there is genuine sentiment by Uihlein that the game has been improved by technology, will free enterprise stand in the way of a game carefully protected by one main component—rules? What if Nicklaus had only had Orlimar in the 1970s? Byron Nelson echoes the sentiment by saying, "We had to play three-quarter shots because of the weight of the equipment. The lighter shafts make a full swing a luxury."

Graphite and titanium are going mainstream, and the shafts are aiding in the departments of flexibility and fluidity. Forget torque and the physics of the golf swing. What manufacturers are doing is big business and good marketing, but it's one rotation short of diabolical. They are sticking toaster-sized club heads on the end of long (44-45-inch) shafts that are featherweight. The average driving distance has shot up the charts.

In the early 1980s, a drive of 300 yards was rarely mentioned at long-driving contests. From 1980 to 1984, the average driving distance was around 250 yards, with the average number of fairways hit at just over 60 percent. Now, PGA Tour statistics give you a "Can't you do any better than that" ranking if you're below 260 yards. The same numbers indicate a success rate of over 67 percent and an average drive of 265 yards. The equipment is now more like a sports weapon. Tinker with persimmon?

Persimmon may as well be an Otey Crisman putter with a wood shaft. Yesteryear was the brassie, yesterday was the persimmon and today is the supercharged torque-driven, toaster- flying bubble shaft with the superlightweight and sticky grip. Sound like a sales pitch? It's not necessary; everyone is gobbling up the technology so they can gain one thing—an advantage.

Nicklaus has witnessed the dawn of an equipment-driven era. "Before I started playing the game, they were playing with wooden shafts and a small ball. And they were even playing with smaller wood heads. I don't know where they are going with the game. They have made the game much easier for the average golfer, and too easy in many ways for the competitive golfer. I certainly think there needs to be a harness on it someplace. You're going to run out of places to play, if you keep letting equipment get away from you," said Nicklaus.

These are not words for Woods, Leonard, Mickelson or Duval. These are words for the peripheral people in the game. The fog of dollar signs has swept across the dew at Augusta, and the golf manufacturers have carte blanche. The rules of golf have defined the game inside the gallery ropes, but the equipment in the bag is wide open.

As the next generation secures its footing for another 100 years of golf, the soft-spike era will be an asterisk next to its early days on the PGA Tour. In 1996, golf courses in America were looking for ways to keep their manicured fairways and greens protected. The controversy quickly turned to the piece of equipment with the most contact with the turf—footwear. The PGA Tour was a major force in the precipitous change. In the early 1990s, soft spikes were something that the members of the Addams Family used for a bed. But since a company called Softspikes entered the scene in the mid-'90s, the number of courses requiring play in the alternative plastic spikes has been staggering.

The PGA Tour has also been a role model in regard to the change. Before the 1996 season, less than a dozen players used plastic cleats. Now, most players have changed their footwear in favor of comfort and reducing wear on the greens. If you're Tiger Woods, they design the shoes after your game. "I went out to Nike and they did a whole research on my swing and how the forces of my weight change in my shoe. They built a shoe that will stabilize my momentum and my weight transfer. It's a traction-control shoe with a neat little design," said Woods.

Ask John Cook, a PGA Tour player representative about technology, and he says something about laptop computers. What started as an idea to create a communication link between the PGA Tour staff and the players has exploded in gigabytes and e-mails. Ninety-nine percent of the players use a PGA TOUR IBM Think Pad for everything from setting up travel arrangements to checking their stock portfolios. Commissioner Tim Finchem and the PGA Tour staff gave every player with a tour card the Think Pad in 1999. Finchem said the Think Pad network "opens up a whole range of new communication benefits. They can even e-mail me directly."

Cook points to Justin Leonard and David Edwards as two of the first players to attack a laptop as a means of staying organized. The ever-calculating Leonard has only been on the PGA Tour since 1994, most of the time with a laptop in tow. A 19-year veteran on tour, Cook is a computer geek beginner. "They (IBM and the PGA Tour links staff) took a totally computer-illiterate person and turned me into someonw who can now turn on and get through a couple of things," Cook said. Plans are to eventually extend the computer technology of laptops to the players on the PGA Senior Tour. Cook is now able to set up his room at the Masters and check out Ohio State football scores on his laptop.

While Cook masters technology at his fingertips, his former college coach at Ohio State, Jim Brown, advises that once the game changes on the professional level, it trickles down to college golf and the mainstream. He insists the single biggest change in the game is the metal driver. "I haven't seen a wood-headed driver in the NCAAs in maybe 10 years. Gary Nicklaus had one here in 1989-90," Brown said. Davis Love and Justin Leonard stayed with persimmon drivers longer than most. Then they won majors with metal drivers in 1997.

Tradition or Technology—the balance is teetering and then comes crashing down. The counterbalance is decidedly toward technology. No more speed grooves, screws holding a wooden insert in place. A driver is a highly sophisticated tool for the ages.

"Not anymore" is the best way to address the no-holds-barred equipment explosion. Give any company the open invitation to invent a club that hits the ball farther and straighter, and voilá! Infomercials on golf equipment have replaced ginzu knives and fitness gadgets. Golf manufacturers have taken on a role similar to that of the banking industry. With Pac Man-like precision, the big guys are eating up the little guys—Callaway buying Odyssey, Titleist buying out Scotty Cameron. Two of golf's oldest equipment makers, Tommy Armour Golf and the Ben Hogan Co., were reduced to price tags gobbled up by TearDrop Golf Co. As the dust settles at the end of the century, corporate manufacturer powers Callaway, Taylor Made, Titleist/Cobra, and now Teardrop Golf are standing tall.

With all the acquisitions, the information superhighway is not relegated to the computer. Cell phones ringing in the gallery are starting to make the tranquility of the PGA Tour sound more like a corporate outing. Leonard said, "It's the people who leave them on and say: 'Hey, give me a call, I'm going to the golf course." David Duval contends that if you're focused, a cell phone, pager, or camera is not going to distract a player from his duty on the course. His attitude is, "Unless you're going to frisk everybody when they come in, stop complaining about it." The controversy over what to do peaked at the 1999 Players' Championship. The distractions didn't seem to bother Duval.

And even though golf equipment is battling the next great idea for firmer abs, the PGA Tour 20-something players are paying attention to the greatest club in his arsenal—his bodies.

Walking down the fifth hole at Pinehurst No. 2 in the final round of the U.S. Open, there was Tim "Lumpy" Herron smoking a cigarette alongside Tiger Woods, who backs up his game with a 19th hole in the weight room. Two different bodies, two different successful approaches to the game. In the second round of the 1992 U.S. Amateur at Muirfield, Herron defeated Woods. Seven years later, they were one of the final groups of the U.S. Open. A match-play event? If you look at results, Woods wins. But, suprisingly, Herron works out on a regular basis, too. Fitness is not exactly a new science, but some of the techniques are now aimed specifically at the game of golf.

One of the pioneers is Alison Theitje. She is currently working with the likes of Leonard, Stewart Cink, Grant Waite, Phil and Amy Mickelson, and two rookies, the PGA Tour's Hank Kuehne and Senior PGA Tour rookie Tom Watson. When it comes to Alison Theitje's concept, some might think she has a better chance of creating fat.

When Theitje, a personal trainer, talks about things like hitting the ball farther and lowering scores, well, she is starting to bend ears along with abs, butts, biceps, and quads. Her goal is to actually get rid of body flubber.

Theitje decided five years ago that the two words—*fitness* and *golf*—could be linked. Golfers have certainly worked out and considered health and fitness to be an important aspect of the game, but not like this. Theitje is taking a new body approach to the game.

"Being in the health and fitness industry 14 years, I couldn't understand why in sports like baseball, hockey, football we could help improve their games and keep them injury proof. And it didn't make any sense to me that no one worked with golfers," said Theitje. Lacking a history in the sport, she started asking questions and getting some mind-wrenching and muscle-aching answers.

"Overall, what I heard was golfers thought lifting weights and strength training would hurt their game, and I just thought that was totally ridiculous," she said with a smile. She mentioned Keith Clearwater, but only like he's a water hazard.

And to get really radical, the 36-year-old Theitje decided what better way to pilot a program than to start at the highest level, the PGA Tour. Enter, Tom Watson. This is the same Tom Watson who was winless on the PGA Tour from 1987 until, he started working out with Theitje. The same 49-year-old who was drifting off leader boards in the early '90s was now 25th on the tour's money list in 1996.

It all started on a winter's day in 1996. Watson contacted Thietje after he played a round of golf with his coach, Stan Thirsk. Watson couldn't believe the 69-year-old's new swing. He was hitting the ball farther, and it was noticeable, of all places, on the scorecard. Watson said he had not seen Thirsk hit a ball like that in years. The next day, Watson phoned Theitje.

Theitje announces proudly: "He was my first PGA client." Soon after that, she started her company, Total Approach Golf, and Watson dropped weight and started winning again. He credits Theitje's training program in large part for his turnaround. "The most important thing for me was how I felt toward the end of my rounds. Fatigue was not a factor," said Watson. Both Watson and Theitje call the Kansas City area, home. "He (Watson) just followed my program, and I knew we had something," said Theitje.

Although Watson was quick to jump on the treadmill, it's hard for Thietje to keep him focused on fitness. "I constantly need to remind him to get back to it," she said.

Please don't get Theitje's program confused with therapy. Therapy is for sissies compared to Theitje's in-your-face fitness program based on—are you ready for this?—the science of muscles and how they function.

Theitje's programs are designed for improving the player's strength, flexibility and stamina. "We customize the program for each athlete. We hit every major muscle group including the biceps, and triceps; we do squats, lunges, plyometric training," said Theitje. Part of her mission statement is really more education, getting the mainstream to link two more words, *athlete* and *golfer.*

Theitje admits to knowing little about the golf swing. Before forming her concept, her closest brush with professional anything was dating former Kansas City Royal Buddy Biancalana. Although she would have troubleshooting anyone's age, she is scoring big points in the fitness corner for her PGA athletes.

For athletes in other sports, this fitness concept is not new, but golf's relationship to fitness has resembled the distance between a titanium-powered drive and a tap-in.

But really thinks she can help players who are in the twilight of their PGA careers. Two players from Texas are high on her list. "I really think I can help players like Tom Kite and Ben Crenshaw, the ones who are getting older," said Theitje.

Theitje still sees Tiger Woods in the gym and at various events, doing a version of what he started for Wally Goodwin at Stanford. "He's seen me around for over a year and he mimics some of things we do in the gym and smiles. He looks up at me and says, 'Am I doing this right, Doc?'" Theitje said.

The scrawny one-iron version of Woods teed off at the Milwaukee Open in 1996. "I think I was 160, 162, somewhere in that range," Woods said. "But now I'm weighing 177. My body fat dropped quite a bit. I've been doing a lot of lifting, and it's starting to pay off," said Woods. The physics of the golf swing rotates around a simple axis, and the net equation is not mind-boggling; it's club-head speed. Ask Tiger Woods about uncoiling his body around and he spits out, "I can unwind my body faster than most players; hence, I can get a whip effect going where I can sling it out there." Like the flamboyant apparel that hit its stride in 1975, the kid born in 1975 has a new fad, getting phat on working out.

What a combination: titanium shafts, a "hot golf ball," muscle fiber, and sleek, green fairways. The kids and the game are Y2K compliant. Will the equipment manufacturers take heed? Or will the ruling bodies of the PGA Tour, USGA, and the Royal or Ancient have to crash the hard drive on where the game is headed?

EN FUEGO

If the world goes dark in 2000, it might not be a Y2K compliance issue. It might be that one of Sergio Garcia's Titleists hit a transformer and began a ripple effect through the entire kingdom of golf. Brookline Ryder cup captain Ben Crenshaw, calls him "magic." The people who have separated the sport from entertainment are calling him "electrifying," introducing the newest member of the masters of the millennium—he might already have a nickname, El Niño, but his game is En Fuego—lightning in a 5-iron. The indomitable Spaniard, Sergio Garcia, is a spark in a petroleum plant, and he's playing lights-on golf.

If the collective foreign 20-something players fail to produce gigantic numbers before they turn 30, there might be a fearless Spaniard who makes some noise, and he has 10 more years to perform. Make no mistake about the way Sergio Garcia plays golf. Like a bullfighter, he's fearless, and he doesn't play that way because of Greg Norman, Jack Nicklaus, or his fellow Spaniards, Seve Ballesteros and José Maria Olazabal. He plays that way because of Tiger Woods. Garcia is quickly turning into the catch-all 20-something phrase and turning the clock back uno ano. At the age of 19, Garcia is not an overnight sensation. He's won more than 70 amateur events, including the 1998 British Amateur.

Since turning professional last April (where he finished as low amateur at the Masters, 38th), Garcia has won the Irish Open at Druids' Glen in Dublin (just his sixth pro event) and scared the likes of Colin Montgomerie at the Loch Lomond in Scotland, finishing in a tie for second. Montgomerie hoisted the trophy and said, "Garcia has raised the bar in Europe just like Woods did in America."

There you have it—confirmation that El Niño is more than just a kid. His only blemish, other than the fact that he has struggled to get his driver's license and a high school diploma, is that he shot 89-83 at Carnoustie to miss the cut. Time will heal that wound, but before the new millennium stretches for its first nap, the Spanish wonder boy may show more guile than the average PGA Tour grinder.

With the 40-something European contingent of Ballesteros, Nick Faldo, Ian Woosnam, Sandy Lyle, Bernhard Langer, and 30-somethings like Montgomerie and Olazabal, Garcia adds a refreshing international flavor to the PGA Tour melting pot.

Don't get Garcia's game mixed up with a hip-hop attitude. He displayed respect and admiration at his first PGA Tour event, the Byron Nelson Classic. Before he teed off in his first pro event, he took off his hat and knelt before Mr. Nelson at the first tee. Garcia said, "I felt he was a legend and a great player, and he's older than me." Nelson is 68 years older than Garcia, but the reverence will get Garcia down the right cart path in better shape than a lot of his 300-plus-yard drives. Garcia finished in third place at the Byron Nelson, which caught the attention of the PGA Tour set. Billy Mayfair said, "He has the whole package."

Garcia has Woods-like charisma, which translates into mucho dinero off the course. Titleist CEO Wally Uihlein inked

Garcia to a multiyear endorsement package and said, "Sergio represents the promise of quality, excellence, and leadership, common characteristics shared with our brands as we enter the next millennium."

As for on the course, his swing has been criticized for its fullness. Can it withstand the pressure of major competition? "I don't think I'm too young to get nervous. But when I was an amateur, it helped me a lot. So, I feel pretty confident," said Garcia.

Like Woods, Garcia has shown signs of brilliance and then signs of lacking experience in the game, such as his play at Carnoustie. Can he hold off the expectations long enough to seize the moment in the new millennium?

As in bullfighting, his scorecard is not as important as his victories.

BEAM ME UP, SCOTTY

Scotty Cameron often woke up on Saturdays because he heard the rustle of the newspaper and his dad in the kitchen. That meant it was almost time to go. As a five- to six-year-old growing up in Orange County, California, in the late 1960s, Scotty Cameron was like a cling-on, grabbing his dad's leg for a scavenger hunt around Fountain Valley. There was no time for Saturday-morning cartoons, T-ball, or a day at the beach. Timing was everything. His father, Don Cameron, would say, "Making the rounds early sometimes separated a good day from a bad day." With Scotty in tow, their destinations would be swap meets, thrift shops, battered driving ranges, and used club barrels in pro shops—anywhere that might turn up old golf clubs. Saturday morning and the hunt was on.

Scotty's father's penchant for golf clubs grew out of his respect for the game. Early on, it served as a common ground for the father to communicate with his young son. "Son, feel the softness of this shaft; oh, check out the forging and, how the lines flow back here." Knowledge of classic clubs that he imparted to Scotty made an indelible impression on him as he grew up. Together they collected hundreds of clubs. Forget Mickey

Mantle's rookie card; this was a quest to collect classic golf clubs. Scotty, now 36, said, "My dad put into my head at such an early age the importance of craftsmanship. It was the little things that made a huge difference. From the paddle grip on Arnold Palmer-design bys, to the softness of the shaft, to the grain of the wood head, to the sole plate. His father, who worked as an insurance investigator in Los Angeles, would say, "Did you notice how some clown put that stamp on that Tommy Armour?"

The two would laugh together at gaffes made by club makers and designers. As Scotty grew into his dad's hobby, the stories became part of their adventures. "Like when Tommy Armour and George Bayer came out with their LFF driver for MacGregor. "This huge-headed, deep-faced driver actually stood for 'let the f—— fly.' The stories behind the clubs were sometimes better than the clubs themselves," said Cameron.

The weekend excursions started out as a fun pastime and became very much an educational event for the younger Cameron. Like any collectors, the two would dig through an old barrel of clubs with blue-collar swiftness, looking for specific artifacts: Tommy Armour persimmon woods, Wilson 8802 putters, and Arnold Palmer design by's. To the Camerons, these were the pearls of the trade.

Once they came home with the big catch, they would examine their goods in the immaculate garage shop with an expanse of tools. "All my friends at school were working after school on their skateboards, bicycles, and getting in trouble. My father and I would actually tinker with clubs and go out and use them in the late evenings," said Cameron.

Then, tragedy struck the Cameron family in 1976, when Scotty was just 13. His father, who taught him so much about golf clubs and even more about life, passed away from a heart-attack.

Shortly after his father's death, he got his first job at Miles Square Golf Course. His job title was "cart-boy." At the course, he was introduced to a local golf teacher named Dan Anselmo. "He (Anselmo) took me under his wing. I recognized him as a craftsman of the golf swing. And as a teenager I was still trying to get proficient at the game," Cameron said. Anselmo's father, John, would later become Tiger Woods' first teacher in the same area of Orange County, California. Dan Anselmo became a big-brother figure to Cameron. As a teen, Cameron was a solid ball-striker, but he said, "I was a psycho with a putter in my hands. I thought way too much." When Cameron wasn't shagging carts and re-gripping and cleaning clubs, he would get a tutorial on putting from Anselmo. Anselmo made the same impression on putting that Cameron's father made on club design. Scotty Cameron, a self-proclaimed "thinker," was channeled into a direction in life.

He had inherited his father's attention for detail and coupled it with his own creativity to sculpt cutting-edge craftsmanship. He took the concept of putting from Anselmo and set out in the real world with high expectations, very much like the 20-some-thing players on the PGA Tour. The difference was that Cameron wanted to put the putter in their hands and let their talent re-ward his craftsmanship. He started designing putters like the Blue Goose for Ray Cook.

By 1994, Cameron's company was in full motion. He was doing design work, manufacturing and milling for several com-panies including Mizuno, Maxfli, and Cleveland Golf. That's when an old friend from Ray Cook golf, Peter Kostis, approached him at the Players' Championship. Cameron and Kostis had de-veloped a friendship when both worked for Ray Cook. It was Kostis who had designed putters for Ray Cook before Cameron joined the company to, as Cameron put it, "pick up where he left off."

Kostis funneled his efforts more toward teaching and commentary work. At this same time, Cameron was busy finding homes for some of the work he was doing for the cadre of golf companies. "At this time, I strictly wanted to make Cameron products and make the finest, Cameron said. "I wanted to make the Ferrari, the Rolls Royce, the Cartier, the Tiffany, or Rolex of putters." But at the Players' Championship, he agreed to take the business card of Titleist CEO Wally Uihlein. The first question Cameron asked Kostis was "Who's this Wally guy?" Uihlein had asked Kostis for an opportunity to meet Cameron with the agenda being that Titleist wanted Cameron to design a putter line for its company. Cameron then told Kostis, "I really am not interested in doing any more work for another company. I am doing my own." Kostis urged Cameron, "Just meet with him. I am going to have him give you a call."

Cameron returned to his putter studio, and on Thursday of the same week, he received a call from Uihlein. They set up a breakfast meeting for the following morning at 8:00 at LaCosta. Breakfast on the patio turned into lunch, and by mid-afternoon, both Cameron and Uihlein had formed a unique relationship. Uihlein had done an uncompromising amount of homework on Cameron prior to the meeting.

"He came with a three-inch-thick folder filled with classified ads I had done as a small company eight and nine years ago, press interviews I did for Ray Cook, quotes and Darrel surveys (surveys at tour events indicating what the players were using). It was unbelievable. He had obviously been watching what I had been doing for a long time, and I was impressed," said Cameron. Uihlein had actually seen Cameron's become the No. 2 putter on the PGA Tour in 1991-92, leapfrogging Titleist, Wilson, MacGregor, and Maxfli. Uihlein, not wanting to stand flat-footed and let the putter market become another range ball in the field, said, "Who is this Scotty guy?"

His young company was beginning to take off, but Cameron admits he was affected by his discussions with Uihlein. A catalyst in his success was Bernhard Langer's win at the 1993 Masters with a Scotty Cameron putter. He chatted with his wife, Kathy, about the direction of their company. Three weeks later, he said to his wife, "You kinda need to meet this guy. Tell me I'm crazy, but meet this guy. He's pretty amazing."

Uihlein made a trip from Fairhaven, Connecticut, back out to meet with both Scotty and Kathy Cameron in Irvine. Their three-hour lunch turned Kathy Cameron's hesitancy into a "Cameron wish list", which was negotiated over time until the two parties (Titleist and Cameron) created "a marriage."

About a year after their merger, Tiger Woods, just a month into his rookie season, approached Cameron about making him a putter. Cameron had done extensive sourcing and work in Japan and recommended to Woods that he try a Scotty Dale putter with the inscription "SLC" on the bottom of the putter. Cameron told Japan customs officials it stood for "Special Limited Cameron," but Cameron always like to incorporate a part of his personal life in his work. During the development of the prototype for the putter, Scotty and Kathy's first daughter, Summer Lynne, was born.

Woods started using the putter with surprising results. Woods never mentioned the inscription "SLC" on the bottom of the putter, after all it did not affect the ball going to the hole. But the real reason the inscription was on the putter was for Summer Lynne, their newborn. At the Las Vegas Invitational, Woods used the putter to edge Davis Love III in a playoff to win his first professional event. Tiger Woods didn't realize it at the time, but he used the Summer Lynne Cameron (SLC)-inscribed putter at the TPC Summerlein. Maybe his trips to the Buddhist altar with his mom, Tida, were beginning to yield some good karma. Woods used the putter again in October to win at Disney.

Woods, forever seeking perfection, decided to switch to a Newport platinum putter early in 1997. As Cameron remembers putting the finishing touches on Woods' "new" putter, he remembers thinking it was incomplete. "I decided to put 32 white dots on the back of the putter, because that was how old I was at the time," he said. Woods used the putter at Augusta in 1997 to put 12 dots between his four-day total and the rest of the field.

To some, Cameron's merger with Titleist might superficially appear to be just another case of a big company gobbling up a smaller company, but Cameron's "marriage" with Titleist created his own tiny universe—call it putterdom. Nowhere in the vast universe of golf equipment manufacturing is anyone doing anything remotely close to what Scotty Cameron is doing on his tiny planet in Escondido.

Woods, Duval, Mickelson, and Leonard all use Scotty Cameron putters. But each player came to find the putter planet in different ways. Cameron calls Mickelson "the most technical" of the foursome because he dissects his own stroke. Mickelson said, "I expect to hook putts, slice putts, and hit putts square." Of the over 130 players Cameron has worked with, Mickelson is the only one who has approached his putting in this frame of reference.

Mickelson was initially not responsive to Cameron's request for a 30-minute consultation. Cameron eyes his prey like a shrink who sees the opportunity to counsel a prospect. As he himself put it, "Some players don't want to learn what they're doing is wrong. I am not here to change things as much as to help them understand the difference." With the exactness of putting, Cameron may now be right behind Bob Rotella when it comes to player confidence.

Mickelson had been working with Jack Burke on his putting. Burke is a revered teacher who has also counseled Steve

Elkington. Burke gave Mickelson a putter and told him, "I think you should use something like this.

Mickelson took Burke's putter and gave it to Larry Watson, the Cameron/Titleist PGA Tour rep. "It was like an old Calamity Jane, and it finally gets back to me," said Cameron. Cameron's disgust was evident. "Boy, why would he want this?" said Cameron. "The neck is about five inches on top, it's really a thick putter. I can make this a lot better because the sweet spot is dead in the heel and high in the heel." Watson said, "No, Phil wants it just like this."

Cameron met Mickelson in the locker room at the Andersen Consulting Match Play event in February. "Just give me 30 minutes," said Cameron. Mickelson and his caddie, Jim Mackay, (Bones) met Cameron that afternoon in the putter studio. The Cameron putter techno lingo started to roll off Cameron's lips as he described Mickelson's stroke. "His putter was made from scratch. It was made from a square block of steel and a round cylinder of steel that was welded onto the heel. I have 17 degrees on the back of the putter, seven degrees on the face, because through impact, he holds a three-degree forward press, no matter what he does. The effective loft for him at impact is four degrees, which allows the ball to go along the ground and not into the ground."

And the average golfer thinks a swing thought is to get the ball from the tee to the green? Titleist may call this the art of putting, but if this is art, what is science?

"IT IS SO HIGH TECH, IT BLOWS YOUR MIND. BUT IT IS SO SIMPLE, YOU LEAVE HERE WITH CONFIDENCE." —SCOTTY CAMERON

The Scotty Cameron/Titleist putter studio is like the Starship *Enterprise*. Putting is not science fiction, but Cameron has taken a simple athletic motion and transformed it into a multi-dimensional sophisticated science. Call Cameron the Captain Kirk of putting, and heads begin to nod in agreement on the PGA Tour, from Brad Faxon to Justin Leonard. Paul Azinger, Tom Kite, Mike Hulbert, Mike Sposa, and Greg Kraft have all left the high-tech laboratory better educated and more in tune with "being the ball."

Sposa called Cameron's concept "the artistic magic" of the game. Kraft referred to Cameron as the man with the "greatest mind in golf." Even newcomer Hank Kuehne learned from guys like Leonard and Faxon that if he was going to play on the PGA Tour, one of his first stops should be the putter planet in Escondido. It's Cameron's blend of creative education that he learned from his father when he was a junior player, coupled with his now-scientific approach that has more than the young players on the PGA Tour in command of 40 percent of their game.

Forty percent of the game is on the green. A breakdown of the numbers shows that the best putters on the PGA Tour average around 28 putts per round. Putting quickly becomes 40 percent of a player's strokes in each round. Can the motion of arms, shoulders and hands command so much reverence? In a game of millimeters, Cameron might be the best-kept secret.

This is the reason the rhetoric inside the Scotty Cameron putter studio is beginning to become PGA Tour putting green chatter. Cameron knows that each player uses a slightly different technique and posture to address and send the ball in motion. Cameron takes the nuances of each player and computes the effect. He uses high-speed videotaping equipment, computers, and lasers for alignment to evaluate the putting stroke. Lie angle, ball position, putter weight, length, loft, and acceleration of the putter are factors that Cameron spits out like he's on cruise control.

There are five cameras set up to catch every angle of the putting stroke. One camera is on the ball, and one is on the shaft. At impact the cameras capture the shaft angle, as well as the ball performance. An overhead camera shows the path. A lie angle camera shows the position of the putter head. Not even the constant buzz of the milling machine affects the brain waves inside the studio. If Tom Kite or Paul Azinger gets lost in Cameron's sophisticated lingo, the machines are there to, "add to the credibility of my message," according to Cameron.

It is easy for Cameron to convince fickle PGA Tour minds of his scientific approach. "When you're standing over a 10-foot putt on 18 to win half a million dollars, a guy should not be worried about his forward press creating too much loft or not enough loft."

Justin Leonard remembers thinking about his putt during the final round of the 1997 British Open. Leonard likes the milled look of his putter because he says it looks like "crushed leather." He said, "I've always putted with a plumber's hosel (where the neck actually makes a right angle and allows the shaft to be over the center of the ball). And Scotty (Cameron) told me he could make a putter for me. He did it, and it's been in my bag ever since."

When Leonard won the British Open in 1997, he credited part of his success to the trust he had in his equipment. "Yeah, on 17 at the British Open, it came in handy," said Leonard. Cameron calls Leonard "a true gentleman in the game" and then trails off into a discussion on his putting stroke, breaking it down into loft percentages, eye position, ball position, and path visualization.

"These young guys on the PGA Tour, 30 years and younger, all have the mind-set that Ping is a soft putter. They missed the era of the Arnold Palmer design-bys, the pencil shafts and a Cashen putter; wonderful feeling cushy putters," said Cameron.

David Duval is one of the players on the PGA Tour who grew up playing junior golf with a Ping putter. Duval went to Cameron and said that Cameron putters were too soft. He asked Cameron if they could use a harder material. Cameron knew this would result in changing the sound of Duval's putter. As he said, "Sound has more to do with feel than feel itself." So Cameron put a slot in the bottom of Duval's putter. The slot created a sound that makes it sound hard. Duval uses a Newport putter that has a slot that achieves a certain "hard noise sound" when it makes contact with the ball.

Mark O'Meara recently asked Cameron to make him a putter identical to Duval's. When Cameron showed up with the Duval look-alike putter at Medinah, O'Meara hit one putt and said, "No, Duval's putter in my length; this is too short."

Before Cameron left Escondido for Chicago and the PGA at Medinah, he finished a putter designed for Sergio Garcia. El Nino had met Cameron at the 1998 British Open, and the young British Amateur champion had asked Cameron to come up with a putter similar to the one he saw in Barry Lane's bag. When Cameron arrived at Medinah, he handed the putter he had styled similar to Lane's to his Tour rep, Larry Watson. Not able to find Garcia, Watson had the club stored in the young Spaniard's locker.

On Tuesday, Cameron was talking to another company tour rep, who said, "Hey, I saw that putter you made for Garcia; it's in his bag." Cameron was incredulous. "It's in his bag? You have got to be kidding me. That was just a thought, it was a first attempt."

Later, on the putting green, Garcia walked over to Cameron and shook his hand. "I love this putter," said Garcia. "There is just one thing, one small thing that I want you to change. There is no mark here over the second "n" in El Nino on the back side."

Garcia held the club up to show Cameron he had forgotten the tilde (ñ—the phonetic indicator).

Garcia used the putter to record 14 birdies over the 72-hole tournament. The Cameron putter also contained the usual Cameron inscription at the top of the club. The initials "JAT" were stamped on Garcia's blade for the first tournament in which he used the wand. The letters "JAT" stood for "just a thought." Cameron had planned for Garcia to test out the prototype putter and have it tweaked for his individual preference. Instead, Garcia was more than just a thought on the leader board Sunday, as he narrowly missed grabbing his first tournament on American soil —a major. And Garcia is more than just a thought as a burgeoning player in the new millennium.

Cameron uses various California cities to identify his putters —Coronado, Newport, Laguna. "I am a big believer in giving a putter a personality. These cities give them an elegance," he said. Elegance was not in mind when Cameron named the Blue Goose putter for Ray Cook. But since it was blue and had a gooseneck, the name fit the image of the putter.

David Berganio Jr. won the 1991 and 1993 U.S. Public Links championship. He also won a national championship with Jim Furyk at Arizona. But after successfully stumbling through the first round of qualifying to gain full exempt status on the PGA Tour, he called the doctor of putting. "Dude, I lipped out every putt today. This is terrible," he said. He asked Cameron, "Can you finish that putter for me? I need a new look." Cameron's response was "What loft do you want?" Berganio said, "Dude, just make it whatever."

Another half-hour session later, an enhancement done by high-speed video showed the Los Angeles native that, in Cameron's words, evidence that "the ball was crashing into the grass, losing speed and direction. I bet you're lipping everything to the right." Berganio said, "You're exactly right."

Berganio was freaking out at the prospect of his own poor physics of putting. He suddenly realized in three days that he would be at the final stage of Q-school. "What am I going to do?" After Cameron milled a putter with the proper loft, he sent Berganio on his way. Berganio's response after he used 26 putts at Q-school and beat the rest of the field by eight strokes? "Dude, the ball looked like it was looking for the bottom of the hole." Problem solved.

Ray Cook, Otey Crisman, Karsten Solheim, George Low, and John Reuter Jr.—all have designed and manufactured putters. "These guys did exactly what I did, but I have a computer system that has helped me prove to players that it is a science," said Cameron, figuring his technology on putting is 15 years ahead of his competition from the manufacturing and design standpoint.

Peter Jacobsen was the first player to sign the wall inside the putting studio. Cameron used to ask the players to sign the wall. Now, players ask to sign Cameron's wall. The wall of golfing fame features hundreds of signatures. One signature stands out as identifying this Cameron genre of golf: "Scotty, Thank you for such a great day. Teach me more. I will be back." The golfer was Hal Sutton.

As the technology improves, Cameron's mark will become even more evident. His perspective on his direction reflects the sense of tradition that he learned as a young boy searching for classic clubs with his dad. He said, "I really just want to continue what others have started."

EPILOGUE

SEPTEMBER IN BROOKLINE (1913)

Frances Ouimet didn't belong at the 1913 U.S. Open at the country Club in Brookline, Massachusetts. He was just a twenty-year-old kid, an amateur. David had better odds of beating Goliath than Ouimet winning the U.S. Open. He could not even make match play in the U.S. Amateur championship. After all, he was just a few years removed from being a caddie on the same course. His own caddie for the championship was a ten-year-old, Eddie Lowery. Why bother to tee-it-up? Two British legends named Ted Ray and five-time British Open champion Harry Vardon came to Boston to claim the U.S. Open and haul it back to England. The only question unanswered was which of the two English players would win?

Somehow Ouimet did not pay attention to the odds. Somehow the only American to have a chance was the skinny kid with an unshakable persistence. Ouimet won the U.S. Open in an 18-hole playoff. He beat Ray and Vardon and the rest of the field at the country club as the decidedly partisan gallery hoisted him on their shoulders. It was not a turning point for golf in America —it was the beginning.

September in Brookline (1999)

Eighty-six years and six days later is a long time, and with the U.S. trailing 10-6 after two hard-fought days of Ryder Cup competition, it is a little difficult to get sentimental when you're getting your red, white and blue butt handed to you by a television announcer and the opportunistic European team. No team has ever come back from that kind of deficit, such long-shot odds. And then it happened. The U.S. team did not listen to the naysayers, they talked about things that grown men don't usually talk about—things like love, fate, destiny, empowerment and courage. They laughed, cried and developed a connectedness with each other that proved to be their strength. They took a "yes we can" approach and responded like any average Ouimet-like player.

It is amazing how a single day on the golf course can create such patriotic drama. The expectations before the event, coupled with their early play, would seemingly create a cacophony of distrust. Captain Ben Crenshaw instilled just the opposite. Crenshaw reminded his team that they had an opportunity. The could fold up their tents or they could combine to be part of something special. The 1999 Ryder Cup could have easily been a year of what ifs and almosts.

A 45-foot dagger of a putt by Justin Leonard was the harpoon. But each of the 12 players strutted their games on Sunday, four of them happen to be the Masters of the Millennium.

The Thursday before the Ryder Cup opening ceremonies, I made two phone calls. My first was to Justin Leonard's mother, Nancy. She sent me some pictures of Justin as a junior player. I called to ask her how old Justin was in a couple of the photographs. I knew that she was in Boston with her husband Larry to watch Justin compete. I had a publisher's deadline and wanted to say something inspiring so that she knew I was behind the teams impending domination. Instead I said, "Thanks for the photographs, I just wanted to ask you a few questions about Justin's age in a few of them. Call me when you get back from Boston." I paused and then slowly hung up the phone. I could not even say a simple "good luck", or even a "go U.S.A."

My next call was to Scotty Cameron. The putting doctor was making a house call to Boston. Something about last-minute changes for some of the Ryder Cuppers. His assistant, Hank George said, "He had a few players from each side who needed adjustment of their equipment." As I hung up the phone it occurred to me that here was a guy who was as American as apple pie and he was jumping on a plane to provide a last-minute "tweak" or ammunition for one of the European players. Talk about your job getting in the way of emotion.

The Ryder Cup is the unofficial end of two years of PGA Tour adrenaline. It also marked the end of this book. When I started the project two years ago, I had six players whom I wanted to feature as they rose from the innocent playground of junior golf. I whittled the group to a foursome in 1999. My foursome did not play well the first two days at Brookline. Leonard, Duval, Mickelson and Woods looked like the Masters of Mass Confusion instead of the Masters of the Millennium.

I went to Sunday school before any of the matches teed off. We talked about the book *Tuesdays with Morrie*. Morrie Schwartz is a guy who looked death in the eye and said, "I am going to celebrate life, you'll have to wait." Crenshaw celebrated Harvey Penick's life with a green jacket earlier in the decade, and now he was the emotional cog behind the U.S. fighting spirit. A team that looked elimination in the eye and celebrated something so rare.

It really didn't matter that Justin Leonard, Phil Mickelson, David Duval and Tiger Woods were filled with woe on Saturday.

In the span of time it takes to play a single round of golf, the PGA Tour's children met destiny head on at the Country Club. The U.S. team played old-fashioned singles golf on Sunday. *Duuvy was groovin'*, the *Mickelsonian way* ended with a 5 and 3 victory, *Woods came back* and showed a cold heart to Coltart and Leonard's game arrived *just in time*. Even the *wind in Furyk's* sail extinguished the Spaniard *En Fuego*.

Golf on Sundays can be so poetic.